Encouraging Your Child's Imagination

Encouraging Your Child's Imagination

A Guide and Stories for Play Acting

Carol E. Bouzoukis

Rowman & Littlefield Publishers, Inc.
Lanham • Boulder • New York • Toronto • Plymouth, UK

Published by Rowman & Littlefield Publishers, Inc.
A wholly owned subsidiary of The Rowman & Littlefield Publishing Group, Inc.
4501 Forbes Boulevard, Suite 200, Lanham, Maryland 20706
http://www.rowmanlittlefield.com

Estover Road, Plymouth PL6 7PY, United Kingdom

British Library Cataloguing in Publication Information Available

Library of Congress Cataloging-in-Publication Data
Bouzoukis, Carol E. (Carol Elaine), 1960–
  Encouraging your child's imagination : a guide and stories for play acting / Carol E. Bouzoukis.
    p. cm.
  Includes bibliographical references.
  ISBN 978-1-4422-1287-9 (cloth : alk. paper) — ISBN 978-1-4422-1289-3 (electronic)
  1. Drama—Study and teaching (Elementary)—Activity programs—United States.
2. Drama in education—United States 3. Imagination in children. 4. Creative ability in children. I. Title.
  PN3171.B634 2012
    649'.51—dc23   2011025886

∞™ The paper used in this publication meets the minimum requirements of American National Standard for Information Sciences—Permanence of Paper for Printed Library Materials, ANSI/NISO Z39.48-1992.

Printed in the United States of America

For J. V., who is on the verge of imagining it all . . .

CONTENTS

CONTENTS

FOREWORD

When Carol asked me to write the foreword to her book, my first thought was, "Wow, that's really cool!" My second thought was, "Uh oh, I'm a TV meteorologist, not a writer." (She knows this—she tells me she was up watching when I worked mornings in Philadelphia: morning infant feedings for her, morning forecasts for me.) Then I thought, "How am I not going to mess up this honor she's given me?"

Then I read her book. It was thoughtful, fresh, and, more importantly, something with which I immediately connected. It is one mom talking to another. I loved that and knew it would be easy for me to tell people why Carol's book is important.

To say this mom has gotten in touch with her inner child recently might be an understatement. You see, having three boys in four years sort of makes that a no-brainer—a must, a responsibility even. I have the joy of watching and learning from the very best: a one-year-old, a two-year-old, and the miniman of the house, my five-year-old. This might be the age I would like to freeze forever in time. Five-year-olds are sweet (at least when well rested), more independent, and smarter with each passing day but still possess that perfect innocence. And it *is* perfect, the right combination and the joining of forces of imagination and reality.

But have you noticed recently that reality seems to be winning more and more? I am not sure which bothers me more: the barrage of inappropriate cartoons or every single toy requiring batteries and the reading of a huge instruction manual to play with it (in his short time on earth, my son has acquired enough skill to operate my iPhone better than I can). I'm unable to shake the feeling this precious early childhood time is slipping away more quickly than it did for me. I find myself wondering whether it is going to be impossible for my boys to hold on to *their* inner child. Am I old-fashioned for wanting that, or is there even a real need for it in our modern life?

This is why I was so thrilled to read Carol's book. I realized that there is a need to hang on; there is a benefit to wanting to continue to nurture our children's imagination. She uses play acting (no frantic cartoons or batteries here!) and familiar stories to get children to open their minds, feel their feelings, and figure out their next steps. For children to have the ability to "loosen up" minds on another level to solve problems is a critical skill. This skill is useful not just on the playground, in the gym, or on the T-Ball field, but also later in life in the workplace.

I also realized that Carol was telling us that to get children to exercise their imaginations (just like a muscle) will get you healthier kids, happy and socially well rounded. Once you have that, a child's possibilities are endless. Who doesn't want that for their kids? I love things that make sense. And Carol's philosophy makes sense to me. I'm a meteorologist—a scientist. Logic is part of my makeup. I also appreciate how she laid out her ideas. It reminds me of a great recipe. (I love to cook.) Follow it step by step, and you are sure to get something nutritious and delicious. But it also allows your special pinches of this and that to make the result all the better. Trust me; kids will happily eat this up!

It is a technology-driven world in which we live, and I fear it may not be giving my children—your children—the tools I know they will need when they find out that restart button does not fix everything. Dr. Carol Bouzoukis has figured out a way to use our children's natural resources to better their lives today and unleash their potential for tomorrow. It is a huge inhale and exhale for us parents, teachers, and leaders. We need to remember what it is that makes kids *kids*, and what makes them great kids: imagination, exploration, and expression. Dr. Bouzoukis's book feels like the "breather" we all need, and just when our kids need it the most.

Maria LaRosa
Meteorologist, The Weather Channel
Mommy

ACKNOWLEDGMENTS

I thank all of the children that I have worked with over the years for their uninhibited willingness to explore the creative process. The journey to become someone new in a faraway place while defeating all obstacles is one of pure imagination. The work, which is our play, would not be possible without the children's natural ability to create. This includes the ongoing support of the parents and the schools. Thank you to all of the parents who granted us permission to share the photographs of their imaginative children within the creative process.

I extend sincere appreciation to Lena Mucchetti, my assistant and program director for Child Drama Workshops, the professional theatre arts enrichment program that promotes the Story Drama Method in Delaware. My gratitude goes to Jacqueline Connell for her gift as our makeup artist over the years. Much gratitude also goes to my editor, Patti Belcher, for her experienced insight. Thank you to Jin Yu, assistant editor, for all of her help.

I especially thank Maria LaRosa for taking time out of her busy life to grace my book with an eloquent foreword!

Thank you most of all to my husband, parents, and family for their continuous support. And finally, a very special thanks goes to my young son for the imagination to come. I can't wait!

INTRODUCTION: IMAGINATION IS THE KEY

"I wanna be. . . . Oh, I wanna be . . . !" shout the children pleadingly. "I wanna be the littlest goat! I wanna be the wolf!" they call out. "Yes," I say, "You can be anyone or anything that you want to be." A feeling of contentment and satisfaction comes over the children as they are about to enter the world of imagination.

Encouraging a child's creativity and imagination today can result in a successful and well-adjusted adult of tomorrow. "A child without imagination is a child lost. Children's imagination is crucial for development and emotional health."[1] Yet children today are living in a sophisticated technological world with advances unthinkable only a few short years ago. Computers, video games, television, and cell phones may be convenient, but they clearly stimulate immediate gratification in children as opposed to imagination.

> Scientific evidence increasingly suggests that, amid all the texting, poking and surfing, our children's digital lives are turning them into much different creatures from us—and not necessarily for the better.[2]

Technology can be unhealthy when it replaces socialization and direct human interaction.

At the same time, schools are increasingly being forced to cut art and music programs due to budgetary constraints. To meet certain standards, schools are task oriented beginning as early as the first grade, which leaves little, if any, time for creativity. "Imagination is the key to mankind's greatest advances, from the arts to the sciences."[3]

As a parent, I find the changes in the classroom and in society alarming. What is happening to our children's childhoods? Some of our concern can be nostalgic. I remember as a young child using a large appliance box as a hideout. I enjoyed it so much that at Christmas "Santa" gave me a walk-in cardboard house. I have such fond memories of hours of fun pretend-playing in that house. The house came with a mail slot in the door, which inspired me to engage my younger brother to be the postman delivering mail to and from the stuffed animal neighbors in the far corners of the basement. We wrote letters and drew pictures inviting all of the toys to come over to join us for a celebration. He delivered the invitations and then slipped the responses through the slot in the door. All it took was the pretend house and some paper and crayons to fuel our imaginations (and a younger brother willing to be directed by his older sister)! Simple, nontechnological items such as these seem to have disappeared from our children's play world.

As an adult, I understand that by encouraging a child's imagination, we promote intelligence. As Albert Einstein reminded us, "Imagination is more important than knowledge. For knowledge is limited, whereas imagination embraces the entire world."[4]

So how do we encourage our children's imaginations? They are not alone in being engrossed by today's electronics. We've showed them the way, after all. We can find ourselves glancing at the iPhone, surfing the Internet at inopportune times, or staring at the television as a remedy for our exhaustion.

Using stories to play act is an excellent way to encourage imagination and creativity in your child. Children's natural inclination to play, and more particularly, their innate ability to engage in dramatic play, perfectly complements the use of stories for creative expression.

The benefits of children interacting within story dramatization are countless. My Story Drama Method, detailed in chapter 1, is the ideal outlet for a child's imagination and creativity. The role exploration that occurs while acting out a story allows a child to experience taking on a new identity. By moving, talking, and thinking like someone or something else, the child strengthens her own identity, simply by stepping into someone else's shoes for a while. The role-playing gives a child the opportunity to create a new story world that never existed before. The art of acting gives the child the ability to imagine all that is new. It creates a fresh experience that lets the child try out greater levels of emotion. It broadens viewpoint and personal repertoire.

In addition, the Story Drama Method can lead to the enhancement of socialization skills, particularly when conducted with a group, simply through the interaction of the roles in the story. Children can explore varying scenarios with a multitude of emotions, all within the pretense of a tale. The group can actually practice social interactions without even realizing it. Moreover, the children have fun while doing so.

Drama aids children in refining their communication skills by providing them the opportunity to verbally articulate and project their voices. They can communicate nonverbally as well through the safety and distance of their new character. Shy children can become quite assertive, and boisterous youths can develop refinement in the roles they design. The use of improvisation, rather than the use of scripts, gives the children the opportunity to create their own words with which to communicate, further enhancing these skills.

The use of the Story Drama Method can also enhance sensory awareness for children. As the imagination is at play, their use of all five senses of hearing, touch, sight, smell, and taste is heightened. A child pretending to be a kitten eating the porridge river must use her memory to imagine the taste and smell of the porridge. As soon as Jack hears the Giant's "Fee, fi, fo, fum," he runs for his life. He hears the Giant's threat, but even before that, he hears and feels the castle floor shaking from the Giant's footsteps. The very art of dramatization and the focus that it requires enhances listening skills. Touch is explored when the three pigs feel the Wolf's huffing and puffing blowing their way. Hansel and Gretel vividly see the candy house through the dense forest as it beckons them to come and sample. The young actors explore all the senses in each tale. The use of pantomime, the art of silent acting, furthers sensory awareness.

The development of emotional expressiveness and awareness are additional benefits of the Story Drama Method. Whether used in the classroom or in the living room, the stories are a wonderful vehicle with which to emote. The nine classic children's stories studied in this book contain elements of anger, sadness, fear, and hope. Loneliness and abandonment, success and overcoming great odds are all running themes in the selected stories. In fact, all of the stories contain life-threatening scenarios. Most end well, except for "The Gingerbread Man" and "The Boy Who Cried Wolf." Emotions run high in the tales, and players have the opportunity to take on different emotions within the parameters of the particular scene. Pretending to cry or pretending to be angry allows the child a chance to experience and be in touch with a diverse array of emotions. A child may be able for the first time to get in touch with his feelings by viewing those feelings through a character's eyes.

Through the implementation of the techniques in the Story Drama Method, a child is able to create a world filled with new physical and emotional challenges in addition to new characters. Developing a live story that takes place long ago and far away frees a child's imagination. The Story Drama Method uses improvisation-based dramatization, where the possibilities are endless and anything can happen. The stories from yesteryear become fresh and new with the young actors fueling the story lines with current ideas. All of the children's ideas are accepted and acknowledged, although you can't utilize all in a single session, particularly when working with a group.

The Story Drama Method permits the expression of creativity in a variety of ways that children can use to explore drama, art, music, movement, and literature all in a single experience. Drama is in the role-playing of the story. Art is the making of simple props and accessories or the face makeup application. Music, while often used to set a mood before the play begins, can be the base for any simple choreography or dance routine added. Creative movement is inherent within role-playing or dance. Literature is indeed the tale itself.

This is why the Story Drama Method is so beneficial in encouraging imagination and creativity—because it is a pure art form at its best. It is child friendly, since children love to pretend. The Story Drama Method is an artistic form of self-exploration, developed for children and therefore to be done in a playful manner. A child has the ability to grow intellectually in the creative process. Children need to play in order to gain mastery of their world. Drama is a structured form of play, yet it allows children to imagine it all within the parameters of the given story. It stimulates raw imagination within the vehicle of the tale.

Contrary to children's typical dislike of anything that is good for them, they happen to love dramatic play. Above all else, dramatic play brings storytelling to life. Rather than reading words on a flat page, play acting breathes life into the characters, allowing them to run, talk, and think, if only for a short while. Play acting the characters from a story brings three dimensions to the otherwise one-dimensional illustrations found in the storybook. In doing so, the child experiences the story firsthand.

This book will explain the method and provide in-depth examples on how to use child drama to expand children's imagination. The Story Drama Method and guide can be utilized easily and successfully by

- parents of children ages three to eight;

- daycare providers;

- after-school staff;

- Sunday school teachers;

- Girl Scout/Boy Scout troop leaders;

- librarians;

- educators/teachers of prekindergarten through third grade; and

- anyone willing to engage in the creative process of play acting with children!

Encouraging Your Child's Imagination is organized in the form of a guide, exploring nine classic stories that have endured for generations. The first chapter fully describes my Story Drama Method, which I have been using successfully and improving for more than twenty years. Readers will learn how to conduct this approach themselves. Parents and professionals can use this method to reach children on both artistic and educational levels. The process works equally well with a group of children or with a single child. This approach can be used in schools, churches, community centers, daycare centers, libraries, or (best of all) your own family room.

Each subsequent chapter contains one of the nine classic stories, beginning with a brief history of the story and its significance for dramatization. Then the story is presented in a format that can be easily read, memorized, or most preferably, acted out by the leader. The stories are my own versions that I have adapted to dramatization. I created a series of questions for each story to elicit creative thinking within each child. The leader can choose which questions would be most useful for any given situation. Each question does not have to be used each time. The leader can ask additional questions spontaneously as the creative process unfolds.

Each set of questions is followed by the story's analysis. The analysis is an in-depth commentary providing insight and direction for the execution of each story. It describes how to navigate the creative waters. Read the analysis for any selected story before the drama session to gain expertise and learn valuable techniques for play acting. At the end of the analysis are easy-to-follow tips that will make the play-making process go smoothly. The tips are drawn from the analysis and are presented in a bullet format for easy access and readability.

The end of each story chapter contains a table that categorizes the story and breaks down each of the play's components. The chart is particularly helpful if the story will be formulated into a story-drama for presentation purposes.

Once upon a time . . .

Appendix A offers a list of additional stories that lend themselves to dramatization. Appendix B provides information for play presentations before an audience. Appendix C describes appropriate and applicable theatre games for young children. In addition, appendix D provides information on drama with special-needs children. While a play presentation is always a fun and rewarding option, there are times when experiencing the creative process with no audience and no props is just as rewarding. This book is equally useful for nonpresentation purposes. The choice is yours.

Let's do a play!

Notes

1. Natalie Canning and Michael Reed, *Reflective Practice in the Early Years* (London: Sage, 2009), 93.

2. Dalton Conley, "Wired for Distraction," *Time*, February 21, 2011, 55.

3. Harvey Karp, *The Happiest Toddler on the Block* (New York: Bantam Dell, 2008), 111.

4. Albert Einstein, *Cosmic Religion: With Other Opinions and Aphorisms* (New York: Dover, 1931), 97.

CHAPTER ONE
THE STORY DRAMA METHOD

The Story Drama Method has evolved over decades of conducting experiential drama groups, and it has been refined and adjusted to be foolproof and productive. It doesn't have to be a big production. Make it as simple or as complex as you want or you have time for. The Story Drama Method can take up an entire Saturday afternoon or just fifteen minutes before bedtime. Acting out a story doesn't mean you have to have a huge space for running and jumping. You can make the hours fly by in a long car trip with story dramas that your children will remember forever. To begin the process, you need the following:

- Space

- Your child or group of children

- Story = drama

- Audience = theatre

The Space

The term *drama* refers to the creative process, and the term *theatre* refers to the product or play presentation. If in a school, the space can be a large group room, auditorium, gym, library, cafeteria, large hallway, classroom, or meeting room. A reasonably sized space that has room to move is best.

"The story is being brought to life!"

If in a classroom, you can push back the desks to make more room. The space should be private, preferably with doors that can be closed so that adults or other children are not tempted to watch before it is presentation time. A private space is important so that the children do not feel inhibited or judged by onlookers. The creative process should unfold in a safe and nonthreatening space. You can even cover windows, if necessary, to ensure privacy. If at home, any large space can be used as well, including a family room, basement, or recreation room. Weather permitting, an outdoor space can also work well if you can section off an acting area or you have a backyard that doesn't have too many distractions. Selecting a space is extremely important. You want to create a space that allows your child's creative process to blossom.

If you are in a facility or institution, any group room or recreation room should suffice. The Story Drama Method has even been explored successfully from the confines of a child's hospital bed. The space must be conducive to creativity—private, has room to move, and has few, if any, distractions. A room filled with games or toys and educational materials will steal the child's focus and can impair the use of the imagination. A large, empty room with a door that closes works well. A room with color on the walls or art displayed is aesthetically pleasing. A carpeted area or rug is very useful as well. Carpet squares are not recommended because they too often inadvertently become projectiles. Once the space is selected or reserved, the same space should be used weekly or on a regular basis.

The Participants

Next comes a cast for your drama. Children can be assigned to a drama group or volunteer for a drama group. You can use the Story Drama Method with one child or twenty children, depending on your needs, where you are, and the time you have available. This method has even been used quite successfully with special-needs children or children with severe physical or psychological challenges (see appendix D). The Story Drama Method is designed to work in a variety of settings with any population of children.

Story Selection

Once you have selected the space and assembled the children, you are ready to pick a story. This guide outlines and examines nine stories that have been dramatized countless times and have been selected due to their applicability to the art of dramatization. Selecting any of these stories is a good place to start. Once you are familiar with this dramatic method, you can start selecting your own favorite childhood or classroom stories to share with your child. You also can create a purely original story with your children.

Presenting the Story

Now that you have selected a story, you can present the story to your children in a number of ways:

- Memorize the story and act it out (preferred).

- Memorize the story and tell it.

- Read the story from a book.

- Have the group take turns reading the story aloud if the children are older.

The best approach is to read a story in advance and put it into your memory using cue cards if necessary. If you memorize the story, you can then act it out for the children without a book or script. This way, the children are watching a play of sorts, and their imagination is sparked. You don't need professional actor training to act out a children's story. Although those with actor training may have better technique and somewhat of an advantage, you can make up for it in enthusiasm.

You can memorize the story and simply tell it to the children, rather than act it out, but your children will much prefer to see the story brought to life through acting. If you are not comfortable acting out the story, memorize the story and tell it rather than simply read it. If you don't have enough time to memorize the story, or if the story is based on witty dialogue, such as that of Dr. Seuss, then read the book to your children. Just use different-sounding voices for each character, and inflect emotion into the words. Ad lib too, if you want.

Materials

Once you have selected the story and you are ready to share with the children, you need to consider any materials you may need. It is actually best not to use any props, accessories, makeup, or set pieces this early in the process. They will be a distraction and can hamper the imagination.

A polished final product can include colorful and coordinated costume accessories when presenting to an audience, even if the audience is a group of stuffed animals in your home. The creative process or exploration of the story through dramatization requires the child's mind to be activated via thought and physical action. The use of props and materials is discussed at the end of this chapter, regarding sharing the creative work in the form of a play presentation. So resist the temptation to use props at this stage.

Narrating

To act out the story for the children, you will take on all of the roles in the story, including that of the narrator. As the narrator, you will tell the tale in an inviting manner. The narration is the glue that holds the story and, ultimately, the young actors together. You will narrate the story when first telling the children the tale and usually will narrate as the children take on all of the story's roles.

The Leader

In addition to narrating, you should try to step into each character within a story using your voice and body: speak in a different voice for each character, and hold your body in a different stance. When you step back to narration, take the original pose of the storyteller and the storyteller's steady and engaging voice. You, as the storyteller, can take on a dozen different roles per story, depending upon the number of characters. Characters may be further differentiated by the tone and emotion of your voice. And you can easily identify the variety of roles simply by saying, for example, "And then the mother said," which clearly individuates each part for the children.

Your voice can become deeper and slower for the Giant, old and scratchy for the Witch, or high and youthful for Little Red Riding Hood. You can add simple physical signs to enhance the characters to help the children determine which character you are. Use a slightly bent spine for the Old Man, an extended claw stretch for the Lion, or tiny movements for the Mouse. One or two physical changes in the body can transform one into a completely different being. Slight changes can differentiate all of the characters in each story and can give the children who are watching some initial ideas as a springboard from which their own creativity can form.

The Pace

You also can control the pace of the storytelling by using inflection and volume. The pace can be increased or decreased dramatically at any given time. In addition, the narrator can give any necessary stage directions to further the story or to help the actors. For example, when you as the narrator say, "And then, the Mouse entered," you give an easy cue to the actors as to their entrances or exits as needed. As the narrator, you can coach the children if they forget their lines or become shy in front of an audience. For example, "And then the magic harp called out for help . . . 'Master, help me!'" You also can offer hints to trigger the characters' verbal response and cover for them when needed. The child can simply repeat the narration if necessary while staying within the structure of the story.

Acting Style

A presentational style of acting is generally used for children's theatre productions. A presentational style of acting is somewhat broad and slightly exaggerated. Bigger than life is the preferred acting style, which lends itself very well to children's stories. The elements of fantasy or magic are well suited for a stylized presentation. The Wolf, for example, is best presented as cartoonish or one-dimensional to reduce the reality of the situation and make him somewhat less threatening to a child audience.

Licking his chops, rubbing his belly, or tiptoeing along can create an antagonist that is effective but not quite so scary. This style of presentation is simply more fun for children.

Use of Pantomime

I highly recommend that you pantomime instead of using actual props. In opening a door, the child can reach for an imaginary doorknob, turn it, and push the door open. Pantomime or acting without the use of actual props encourages imagination. If Baby Bear is eating a bowl of porridge, he must pick up an imaginary spoon, dip up a spoonful of porridge, and eat it, complete with chewing and swallowing. An old woman rolling out the cookie dough with her rolling pin must do it with her imagination. What would this feel like if she had an actual rolling pin? Let's imagine. When the old man runs up the hill while chasing the Gingerbread Man, he tilts back slightly and can run in place to represent going up a hill. He can hold his back or wipe his brow, yet it is all imagined, no actual hill necessary. You should encourage pantomime for both the initial storytelling and for the children's work.

The Rules

Before acting out the story for a group of children, you need to mention a couple of rules to ensure order. Simply no talking during the storytelling, and whoever does the best listening, particularly with younger groups, will get the first choice in role selection. These two warnings work very well. Due to the unpredictability and impulsiveness of creativity, it is helpful to set up a few simple parameters from which children can benefit. Another useful tip is that the title of the story should not be mentioned until the whole story is over—"And that was the story of Hansel and Gretel"—because this adds an element of recognition and builds momentum.

Casting

Once you have shared the story with the children, it is time for casting. You will hear, "I wanna be the . . . Oh! I wanna be the . . ." Have the children raise their hands while remaining seated in a semicircle to dissuade calling out. It is best to leave the distribution of the roles up to each individual child when working with young actors. Let each child select who in the story he or she would like to be. They can be any person, animal, or thing, and you should mention this to them before they make a selection. It is a bit of a balancing act, but select children one by one to discover which role they have picked to play. As they select the roles, you can suggest any roles that haven't been filled yet, in case you already have six Goldilockses and just one bear. In addition, inanimate roles may or may not be obvious to the children as choices, so you can suggest to them, "Would anyone like to be the river or the tree?"

If any roles go unselected, you can easily step in and play these parts. It is very important to let the children be whomever they want to be, as opposed to the more traditional casting method where the director picks the parts for the children to play. Another rule can be used most effectively to keep the process running smoothly: "You can't trade." Once the children pick their parts, they can't change their minds. Otherwise, some children will change their minds repeatedly, which tends to hamper the process. The child can play an alternate role if time allows reenacting the story again.

When you use this process at home with one or two children rather than with a large group, the child may still select any part that he would like to be but now has the option to select more than one role to play. If he selects only one role to play, then you need to play the other roles to make the story flourish. Some children prefer to play just one part, and that's fine.

As the casting process takes place, a child might select a character to become that is not actually in the story. You should try to fill all of the primary characters first by saying, "A puppy would be a great idea, but first, let's make sure we have a Papa Bear." Try to get most of the primary roles filled by children who want to be in the parts, and then add specialty roles into the story as long as it follows the original character's purpose. It is helpful to maintain the structure of the story and be true to the characters in the story. If a child wants to be a dinosaur, you can usually find room in the tale to encourage your child's imagination. Sometimes, you may want to create a completely original story with all original characters, but this does take more experience as the backbone of the established story is no longer there for support.

If a boy wants to be the part of the mother, that's okay, and you should dismiss any giggling. If a girl wants to be Jack, she can be either Jack or Jackie, her choice. Therefore, the parts are gender neutral. If two children want to be Grandmother, then have two grandmothers in the play. Whether the boys want to be fairies or the girls want to be wolves, all choices should be accepted in a respectful and supportive atmosphere. The children need to be positive and nonjudgmental, and you may need to remind them as a group. If someone chooses to be the narrator, fine, as he may or may not need prodding or coaching. Sometimes, a very shy child will come out of her shell and become more assertive in a role. You should support this. If a child starts to become particularly disruptive or unruly, she may have to sit out temporarily and not get to play a part. Usually, if given a chance to role-play, children can channel their impulsivity into the character in a productive way. They generally want to do well and are motivated by the process and their peers because it is naturally fun.

Characterization

As the children select their parts, they are placed one by one into the story for the opening. I often start with any groups of characters—billy goats, pigs, children—sleeping, as a great way to set the stage. If the children are asleep, the rest of the casting can unfold and the children can have a quiet moment to be in control of themselves. This works wonders when presenting as a play, too. Use a chair to represent Mom's place in the kitchen or as any other central point where applicable. A simple chair establishes location and gives the children a place to focus their energy.

Once the cast is placed in the designated acting area, an optional warm-up phase can begin. Selecting one character or group of similar characters at a time, you should have the children move as they think that person, animal, or thing would move. Horses, for example, could graze or prance, canter or gallop. A giant could move slowly, yet in a big way. Each created character will have a new way to move. Once the child moves as the newly created character, you may explore the voice the child will use. You can allow the children to sound the way they think that the character would sound—the lion's roar, the cow's moo, or the grandmother's gravelly voice. The children can experiment with various voices for their

17

individual character. You should allow everyone to practice saying a line of dialogue before doing the story as an ensemble.

To help the children further with the development of their characterization, you can suggest motivations to help their acting become believable. How does the Wolf act when he is hungry? When was his last meal? How does the Lion act when he is angry? Why is the Lion so mad? You and the children can explore these examples physically and vocally. How does the littlest pig react when the Wolf blows down his straw house? Helping the child discover the attitude of his or her character will also be beneficial in developing the characterizations. Is the Wolf sneaky? Is the boy who watches the sheep bored? Why is he so bored? You and your child can explore any changing emotions within any given role, too. Children can often identify varying attitudes and enjoy role-playing with attention to them.

In the story "Jack and the Beanstalk," the mother is so happy when she learns that Jack sold the cow. When she finds out he sold Bessie for beans, she gets quite angry. The child playing the part of Mom goes from happy to angry very suddenly. Children can pretend varying emotions and changes in emotion if they are given the opportunity to do so within the role-playing. Always remember to point out how the characters appear to be feeling and why. This allows children to be in closer touch with their own emotions while developing characters with some depth.

Subtext

To encourage a child's imagination, you can explore the subtext of the story, which is the psychological motivations of the characters, as well as the backstory. You can trigger the child's imagination by asking some questions about the untold story. Where did these two hunters come from? Did you know that the Giant had stolen all of his riches from Jack's dad many years ago?

The Magic Begins

The casting has been completed, and the initial exploration of the characters is done. You may want to turn off the lights in the room to cue the actors to prepare to begin. You can start the story in a freeze or tableau.

Have all of the children frozen in their individual character pose. The narrator begins by turning the light on and saying, "This is the story of . . ." The actors come to life as their turn arises. Remind the younger children that when acting out the story, they must take turns and wait patiently for their part. They cannot all act at once or else chaos will ensue. Everyone has a role, and the ensemble work begins. The acting group is a team. If by chance a child doesn't want to be in the play and will not choose a part, which does happen (albeit rarely), he can be the audience that day and sit and watch. You should try to encourage all the children to participate, but do not force them to play a part. Perhaps a child would like to be the assistant director instead.

Coaching

As the narrator, you tell the story and encourage and coach the children to play their parts. As previously noted, the narrator can direct the children as the story unfolds. Some children need little, if any, direction, and other children will need some guidance, so remain flexible and aware. Some children can create improvisational monologues, while other children may not say a word. Either extreme is acceptable, and you should encourage and support them. The narrator can describe the entrances, movements, and even coach the dialogue of the young actors: "The Lion yawned and stretched and let out a hungry roar." Describe what the child is to do or may already be doing as the story is enacted. Children are encouraged to make up their own words for the story, which they can easily do, having just heard the story in its entirety. Since the children create their own dialogue, they can better remember their very own words. You can help them as needed. Scripts are unnecessary and often result in stiff performances. This approach is much more playful and natural for children, and it allows for beautiful results.

You should tell the story and coach the children's parts in an improvisational manner, using no book or script whenever possible. If you forget a part of the story, the children will often remind you of the missed part. If time doesn't allow you to put the story to memory, you can refer to the book or create cue cards. If the role-playing gets too chaotic or the children become unglued, simply freeze them like statues to maintain control. Creating story dramatizations does elicit energy and enthusiasm. A group of one kind of character may want to speak in unison, which is helpful as they cue one another about what to say.

Privacy

No one outside of the actors and narrator should watch the creative process work at this stage, as this can cause inhibited behaviors. Only you and the children participate until the presentation day. The creative space should be a safe place for children to experiment and try on different roles. Children will sometimes imitate your interpretation of the characters but are often able to create their own rendition, given the freedom to explore and make their own choices. There are no right or wrong choices in drama, and new ideas are welcomed.

Variations in Casting

In some cases, a child may volunteer to play two parts when the story is being dramatized if there is a part that no one has selected. You should encourage this. Sometimes, as the story is being acted and is nearing the end, the children may all want to become something collectively, such as the river, or the gingerbread house coming to life. You should stay flexible within the story and remain open-minded as to how the process should evolve. Each story dramatization is unique; no two enactments are ever the same. Let the children try their ideas. The story is being brought to life. The live dramatic piece has never existed before and is purely original. The children don't require specific acting lessons, as they are natural at pretending and imagining. The exploration of movement, voice, and characterization is simply integrated into their play. You can explore some specific acting techniques for presentation purposes. It is fun to end each run-through of a story with a curtain call. Everyone (the cast) holds hands and faces front to where an imagined audience could be. The children, while holding hands, can lift their arms up in the air and then down as they bend their waists and repeat. Children love a curtain call, complete with earned and deserved applause. They enjoy this with or without an audience.

If time permits, the children can act the story again and change parts or remain in the same part. Often, the children become more relaxed and more familiar with the story upon reenacting it a second time, and children are drawn toward repetition.

Wrapping Up

You may find it interesting to regroup after the acting of the story and select a specific slice or segment of the story to examine more closely. Ask the children what their favorite part of the story was. Then, with everyone sitting in a semicircle, have one child volunteer to come up and act out one small part of the story with you, a one- or two-minute scene with the rest of the group watching. Then, get a second volunteer and act out that moment from the story again to see whether this second volunteer has a different interpretation or interaction. Do one short scene two or three times, and then select another favorite moment to highlight. Children enjoy acting with an adult, as it encourages their creativity through the exchange. It gives the children a chance to try different parts and to be in the spotlight too. Theatre games and warm-ups can be used in addition to the Story Drama Method, and I've outlined them for you in detail in appendix C.

Benefits

The creative process in which the children participate is where the artistic and emotional growth occurs. The dramatic interactions of the Story Drama Method are in and of themselves significant and so meaningful for the child. Children can play act while creating an original story drama. Their imaginations are triggered, and when play acting in a group, the socialization benefits can be excellent. Peer relations and interactions are explored through the role-playing. Emotions and actions of the characters are understood and played out. The world of pretend for children is of the utmost importance as they learn how to gain mastery of their own world by way of exploring a world in story format. The dramatic process is in and of itself a means to an end.

Staging

In some situations, one of the goals of the process may be to culminate in a production. You can present a play production to an audience at a school or hospital or at home. The formal sharing of the story drama is doable but requires some preparation and forethought. The space where the presentation is to take place should be a space where children have had the chance to rehearse at least once or twice, if not for the duration of the process. A stage is not necessary, as it often swallows up young children and can make it difficult to hear their small voices. You could use the apron (the front of the stage) or even at the audience level in front of the stage on the floor. Any open space can be used as a stage; just be sure, if you are setting up chairs, to alternate or stagger the chairs so that people in the audience can have a clear view.

Audience

The audience can be parents, teachers, staff, and most importantly, children. If at home, one can have stuffed animals as an audience. Or the children can present the play to parents, grandparents, or extended family. Don't allow anyone to watch the rehearsals leading up to the presentation, as you may find overly eager parents and grandparents wanting to take a sneak peak.

Rehearsals

When working with younger children, you should have three or four rehearsals at the most. You want to retain spontaneity and freshness for the play. Any more rehearsals will not hold the attention spans of the children and are not necessary. Older children can have more rehearsals, depending on the desired results and level of polish required. The basic Story Drama Method requires only a few run-throughs to familiarize the children with the story and the scenarios. A few rehearsals will give the cast a chance to create some improvisation-based dialogue and review any entrances or exits. Whenever possible, you should have all young actors placed in the acting area as the story begins, as opposed to any backstage places. With one leader, the children all need to be within view at all times.

Performance Rules

For presentation purposes, you should remind the actors to "cheat out" and face forward toward the expected audience. This technique is not natural in children's play, so you may need to gently position the children as the story unfolds if they turn their backs completely to the audience. Do this so that the audience can see and hear the children. This need not be achieved consistently but is helpful at times.

A few performance rules will be helpful:

- "Cheat out," or face front.

- Don't look directly at the audience's faces, but rather at the clock on the wall (or any point over the audience's heads).

- Speak clearly and loudly—project.

- If someone forgets a line or says something differently, don't correct them.

- If someone loses his or her ears or tails (or costume piece), quietly pick them up.

- Don't break character.

- Don't wave or say hi to Mom and Dad.

- If you forget your line, just look at the instructor, who will cue you or simply say the line for you.

- Stay in the story.

- Have fun!

These rules are helpful for performance day to ensure that everyone has a positive experience.

Costumes

Costume accessories add to characterization for presentation time. You can use ears and tails for animals, an apron for Mother, a cap and vest for the salesman, and a feather boa for the bird to represent wings. See appendix B for suggestions. You can find accessories around the house, and others can be ordered via the Internet. I don't recommend full costumes, as they aren't necessary. It is more conducive to creativity to have the children wear or bring the color of their character for presentation day and then add an accessory or two. This stylized accessorizing on a basic color leaves more to the imagination. A child playing the part of a dog may choose to be brown, black, or even purple. The choice is his to make. You should make an accessory or two available to each child whenever applicable. All of the stories I've presented in this book need only simple accessories.

Props

The children should also pantomime the props because this also encourages them to use their imagination. In addition, young actors can drop props, turn them into weapons, or use them for tug of war. Nonetheless, some objects are useful in telling the story, and I've suggested some easy props in appendix B.

Makeup

When presenting to an audience, children love to wear face makeup. Even a few simple markings as whiskers for the Mouse or a black dot for the Wolf's nose will suffice. Stage makeup in bright colors for children can be purchased over the Internet and washes off easily with soap and water or cold cream. If the budget allows, you can hire a professional artist to paint the children's faces or find the support of an art teacher. Once the makeup is applied, the children are further encouraged to be in character. Some children may refuse to wear makeup; you should not force them to wear it.

You may choose to do a quick run-through just prior to the performance, but don't drain the children's energy. Once the rehearsals are finished, the costume accessories are on, the makeup is applied, the play rules have been stated, and the place has been secured, it is time for the audience members to take their seats.

Presentation Day

Take the young cast to another room as the audience arrives. A smaller audience is more intimate and less threatening. Remind the audience to turn off all cell phones. Distribute a program. It is helpful to have extra safety pins, bobby pins, and wetnaps on hand. Turn down the lights as the child cast enters the room, and then it is lights up and story drama time!

During a live presentation with children, anything can happen, so it is important to stay reasonably calm and make sure to support the children in their creative journey during this, the sharing stage of the method. Sometimes children become very introverted and shy during the play, but generally, they will feed off the leader's energy and work collectively as an ensemble. The important thing to remember is that the story is the structure that carries the characters from situation to situation. All ends well when the plotline's conflict is followed by resolution. Keep the play filled with physical action and movement. The plays need to be primarily visual while being glued together with narration. The dialogue simply furthers the story. The curtain call adds closure and is time for deserved applause. The children can announce their names and their characters' names at the end of the curtain call: "My name is ___, and I played the ___." Then it is time for the children to mingle with the audience (particularly if it is made up of parents) and take some photographs. If a child's parents could not attend due to a prior obligation, be sure to prepare the child in advance. You should take a picture or video of that child if other children are having their picture taken.

This creative approach provides a positive experience for everyone involved. You must execute it in a sensitive and supportive manner. Children respond best to a gentle yet directive approach, as I have described above. As long as some simple rules are in place, the creativity can begin. It is content within form. The following chapters are a guide for play acting. I've selected nine classic stories and analyzed them for you and your children to reenact.

THE WOLF AND THE SEVEN KIDS

"The Wolf and the Seven Kids"[1] is also known as "The Wolf and the Seven Young Kids." This tale was written by Jacob and Wilhelm Grimm, otherwise known as the Brothers Grimm. "The Wolf and the Seven Kids" was first introduced in the Brothers Grimm book *Children's and Household Tales*, published in 1812. A second version was later printed in a slightly different manner in a future edition of *Children's and Household Tales*. This story has motifs reminiscent of both "Little Red Riding Hood" and "The Three Little Pigs," but it never rose to their height of popularity.

"The Wolf and the Seven Kids" has always been a favorite story for children to act out. The children "goats" find themselves home alone when Mother goes off to the market one day. Imagine the excitement when the Wolf comes to the door pretending to be Mother. Chaos erupts once the Wolf sneaks his way inside, including a chase scene! But due to Mother's quick thinking, all are safe and sound by the end of the tale.

"Our mother doesn't have a voice like that," cried the young goat.

The Story

A long time ago, very far away, there lived a mother goat and her seven goat children. One morning as the children all lay sleeping, Mother called them down for breakfast. "Children, children," she cried. The children slowly woke up, yawned and stretched, and then came downstairs. "Children," Mother called, "Time for breakfast." So all of the children sat down in front of Mother for breakfast. Mother said, "Here you are. I have some hay, porridge, and tin cans for you. Now eat up, for I have something very important to tell you." "Yes, Mother," said the goat children. "Today I will be going to the market," said Mother, "and while I'm gone, don't let anybody in unless it is me. Do you understand?" "Yes, Mother," said the goat children. And with that, the mother goat got up, put on her coat and hat, took her purse, and hugged the children goodbye. "Goodbye, Mother," cried the goats. The mother went out the door and shut it behind her, and she was gone.

Well, while she was gone, a mean, old, sneaky Wolf crossed over to the goats' house because he was hungry for goats. He knocked on the door, and the goat children said, "Who is it?" "It's your mother," said the wicked old Wolf in a gravelly voice. "Our mother doesn't have a voice like that," they cried. "Drats," the Wolf said with clenched fists while stomping his feet. The Wolf stomped away disgruntled and very mad.

He went to the store to buy some honey. Then the clerk turned and saw the Wolf in his store. "Oh, wh . . . oh, wh . . . a wolf in my store . . . say, oh, wh . . . Mr. Wolf. What do you . . . need today . . . anything . . . yes . . . and anything you want," the clerk said, stuttering. "I want honey," demanded the Wolf. "Oh, yes . . . of course, honey for you and no charge. Take it with you! Please, don't hurt me," cried the clerk. The Wolf grabbed the honey and left the store. He tilted his head and poured the whole jar of honey down his throat: "Gulp, gulp, gulp," said the Wolf as he drank all of the honey and threw the jar aside. He licked his lips, brushed off his hands, and started back to the goats' house.

The Wolf knocked on the door of the goats' house a second time. "Who is it?" cried the goat children. "It is your mother," said the Wolf, this time with a sweet, soft voice just like Mother's. But some of the young goats peeked through the small window of the door, saw the black, dark, hairy paw of the Wolf, and cried, "Our mother doesn't have a paw like that!" "Drats!" yelled the Wolf. Once again, he clenched his fists, stamped his feet, and stomped off.

This time the Wolf stomped over to the baker's shop. The baker was busy baking when he turned and saw the big and oh-so-evil Wolf. "Uh, oh . . . oh . . . a wolf in my store . . . yikes . . . oh, please don't hurt me . . . oh, no . . . anything that you want . . . anything at all! Oh, nooooo," called out the baker. "Gimme some flour . . . now!" demanded the Wolf. The baker jumped with fear but did give the Wolf just what he wanted, a big tin of

31

flour. The Wolf grabbed the flour and left the store. He opened the tin and proceeded to pat the flour all over his paws and arms, so he was now soft and white. He tossed the tin away and stomped back to the goats' house for the third and last time.

The Wolf knocked on the door. "Who is it?" cried the goats. "It is your mother," said the Wolf with a soft voice while carefully showing his new, white paw through the window. "Mother's home!" screamed the goat children in glee. And they opened the door. The Wolf leapt into the house and roared. The goats ran! One hid in the bathtub. One hid under the table. One hid behind the sofa. One hid in the grandfather clock, and one hid in the sink. But the Wolf was very sneaky and very hungry and, one by one, the Wolf found the goats and gobbled them up. One by one, the Wolf ate up all of the little goats. The Wolf was very full and very happy. With that, he slowly walked out of the house. That mean, old, sneaky, and now full Wolf walked toward a very large tree. He yawned and stretched, feeling quite full. He rubbed his belly and sat down under the tree to take a rest. The Wolf fell fast asleep.

Well, just then, Mother came home from the market. As she neared her house, she saw that the door was ajar. "Uh, oh," she thought to herself. As she went inside, all was very quiet, and there was no one home. "Children," Mother called. Silence. "Oh, children, where are you?" It was completely silent. Just then, the grandfather clock struck one. The cabinet door opened, and out came the littlest kid goat. "Mother, Mother! All my brothers and sisters were grabbed up! The Wolf was here! He tricked us!" the little goat cried. "Listen, quickly get my needle, thread, and scissors," urged Mother, "Hurry!" With that, the littlest goat ran to find needle, thread, and scissors for his mother. "Yes, great," said Mother, taking the items from the youngest goat. "Now follow me, quickly and quietly!"

The kid goat followed his mother out the door, down the path, and toward the woods. There they saw the Wolf.

He was fast asleep under the tree. Mother took her scissors and snip-snip-snip cut open the Wolf's belly. Suddenly all of the young goats jumped out of the Wolf's belly and jumped for joy. "Ssshhh," said Mother, "yes—you're safe. You're fine now." Mother motioned to the children to quickly yet quietly go to the nearby stream and pick up the largest rock that they could possibly carry, and then bring it back to her. The young goat children all ran down to the stream and found the biggest rocks that they could carry. One by one, Mother took the rocks and placed them into the Wolf's open belly. Then quickly she took her needle and thread and sewed him up. "Hurry children, let's go back to the house," cried Mother. So the goat children and Mother ran back to the safety of their house. They went inside and locked the door. From their house, they watched as the Wolf slowly woke up. He stood up, yawned and stretched, and then grabbed his belly and exclaimed, "Oh, I'm so full. I feel as if I ate rocks. I'm so thirsty." Then the Wolf walked over to the lake and bent down to take a drink. Suddenly, he fell head over heels, heels over head, down—down—down to the bottom of the lake. And do you know that the mean old Wolf never ever bothered anyone ever again? And the kid goats cheered and jumped for joy, for they would live happily ever after.

And that is the story of "The Wolf and the Seven Kids."

"Mother, Mother, I hid in the grandfather clock!" cried the youngest goat.

Questions

- Who can be the best kid goat pretending to be asleep?

- Do goats snore?

- Who can slowly yawn and stretch as you awaken?

- How do you pretend to walk down the stairs?

- What do the goats eat for breakfast?

- Can you form a semicircle around the Mother Goat as she feeds you?

- Let me hear the goats eat.

- Can you say, "Yes, Mother," all together?

- Can Mother Goat pretend to put on her coat using pantomime?

- Can you pretend to "air hug" Mother Goat goodbye?

- How do the Goat Children feel when Mother is leaving?

- What can we use to be the door? Can we use this chair to be the door?

- How mean and sneaky is this Wolf?

- How does a mean and sneaky Wolf move?

- How can you tell that the Wolf is hungry?

- Do the goats see the Wolf at the door?

- How do the goats know that the Wolf is not their mother?

- How afraid is the store clerk when he sees the Wolf?

- Can you pretend to gulp down a whole jar of honey?

- How did the Children Goats know that the Wolf was not their Mother the second time he came to the home?

- What does the Wolf do next?

- Is the baker scared of the Wolf?

- When the Wolf finally got into the house, how scared were the young goats?

- Can you think of some other good hiding places for the goats?

- If you don't want to be caught and gobbled up by the Wolf, can you hide behind me, the grandfather clock?

- If the Wolf finds you and tags you, can you curl up into a ball?

- How can we tell that the Wolf is full and happy?

- If you are behind the grandfather clock, are you safe from the Wolf?

- If I am the tree, can the Gobbled Goats hide behind me as the Wolf sleeps?

- When Mother arrives home, how does she know something is wrong?

- Who can be the sound of the grandfather clock striking one o'clock?

- How would the grandfather clock striking one sound?

- How many safe littlest kid goats do we have?

- Can you hide behind me as the grandfather clock and jump out when the clock strikes one?

- How upset is the littlest kid goat after what has happened to his brothers and sisters?

- For what three things does Mother ask?

- Who wants to run and find the needle?

- Who can get the thread?

- Where are the scissors? Can you find them?

- Can you quietly tiptoe behind Mother?

- Why does the littlest goat need to be so quiet?

- Where do they find the Wolf?

- What is the Wolf doing under the tree?

- How can we tell that the Wolf is asleep?

- How can Mother pretend to snip open the Wolf's belly? Can she pretend it in the air?

- Let's see the kid goats jump out of the Wolf's belly.

- Can you jump for joy?

- How did the kid goats feel to be out of the Wolf's belly?

- Can you quietly tiptoe to the water's edge?

- Let me see how you carry a really big rock.

- Can we see how heavy the rock is?

- How can Mother place the rocks in the Wolf's belly without waking him up?

- Can Mother Goat sew up the Wolf's belly in a pretend way?

- How fast can the goats run back home?

- Can I see someone lock the door?

- What wakes up the Wolf?

- How does the Wolf walk with a belly full of rocks?

- Let's see how the Wolf can tumble into the lake.

- Does someone want to be the lake into which the Wolf falls?

- Let me see how happy the goat family is.

- Will the Wolf ever return?

- How does this story end?

Exploration

When a story begins with "A long time ago and very far away," as most fairy tales do, the child is given an immediate feeling of much-needed distance. Stories that include menacing wolves that gobble up small animals/children must begin with the premise that although this did happen, it was long ago and far away. This parameter offers safety and relief to the young listener.

You can tell the children that a kid is the name for a young goat. Girl goats are nanny goats and boy goats are billy goats. The number of kid goats in the story is seven. This can be adjusted to the needs of the group. You can have as many or as few as the group warrants. The number is flexible.

As the story begins, the kid goats are sleeping. This is a wonderful dramatic technique to incorporate into any story. When a story begins with the children sleeping, it is a way to control the group, as children love to pretend to be asleep. As they sleep, they are positioned quietly and are in a still place. It is also a great way to regain control if a group of children gets overly rambunctious. When encouraging children to be creative and use their imaginations, you must have certain parameters at your fingertips to keep the fun within bounds.

You can add interesting moments by having one or more of the goats snore. They can snore individually or in unison. Also, the children can add their legs raising and falling with the snoring for a comic touch. Usually repeating three times is sufficient. The children pretending to sleep also may trigger their subconscious minds to stir, resulting in more creativity during their play acting.

As the children awake "yawning and stretching," again you can describe the action slowly. Slow motion is another great way to keep the children slightly more controlled and in the moment. Slow-motion acting can be utilized in other instances as well. This dramatic technique can be incorporated in group work during any chaotic or climactic scene that could otherwise quickly become out of control. Children also love acting in slow motion. In addition, you can fast-forward any dramatic movement for effect.

You can use simple mime skills to have the children coming down the stairs. They can pretend to hold onto the railing and step down as their hand moves down the imaginary railing. It helps to have the Mother Goat sitting in a chair for blocking (stage directions) purposes. Then when she calls to her children, they can sit in a semicircle around her feet. The children can be directed exactly where to go to sit through the narration. Facing Mom gives the children a focal point.

When Mother feeds the kid goats, you will find that children generally enjoy pretending to eat. This moment can be reflective of nurturance. You will find that the children in need of more nurturance will often inhale their pretend food and ask for more. Give them more. Let them enjoy the interaction of Mother feeding her children. At this point, you can incorporate a "neighing" into the dialogue, for example, "Baa, baa, yes Mother, baa, baa." Most young children love pretending to be animals. You can add the baaing to their voices, and you can encourage specific animal movements as well. Children will enjoy moving around on all fours, and you should encourage them to do so. You can always take a moment before each story begins to let the children practice their animal sounds and movements.

The animals in the story are clearly humanized and can be stylized as such. The children in the role of animals can obviously use dialogue. However, if the children are young and shy, they may be much more comfortable just using the animal sounds without human dialogue. This is fine. In group work, you will find that some more assertive children will naturally do more of the dialogue while others are content with making sounds. Never force a child to say dialogue if he or she chooses not to. However, one useful technique is to have the children talk in unison. This gives them a comfort zone for speaking and security in knowing that some of the children will remember what to say and others who miss their cue will follow along. Speaking in unison takes unnecessary pressure off an inhibited child.

Notice that the story has no father character. Many fairy tales are written this way. Think of "Little Red Riding Hood," "The Three Little Pigs," and "Jack and the Beanstalk," to name a few. Obviously, with today's broken homes and high divorce rate, to have a single parent in the story can clearly speak to a child's needs. Also, with parents having busy careers and often working long hours, one parent in the story can be appreciated by many of today's children. You may want to allow the children to decide whom to add to "their" story when it is time for them to enact it. You can have two or three moms or add a grandparent or a mom and dad, depending on their requests. It is also acceptable to let a boy play the role of Mother if he chooses to. But you wouldn't cast a boy in the role of Mother unless he requests it. Usually, you then have to quiet some giggles from the group. But it is imperative that you let the children be anyone or anything they want to be, regardless of gender, as it is quite harmless.

Then Mother tells the children she is going to leave them and go to the market. This situation can suggest separation anxiety for some children. Children can work through separation anxiety by acting out being left alone by Mother. Children often dramatize being left, for example, as a way of combating this issue. In this story, the child is left with siblings, but Mother's safe and secure presence goes out the door as Mother goes to market.

Not only is Mother leaving them home alone, she also warns them not to let anyone in while she is gone. Naturally, the warning is observed, but eventually it falls by the wayside, as in any good cautionary tale.

Again, "Little Red Riding Hood," "The Three Little Pigs," and "Jack and the Beanstalk" are also cautionary tales, wherein the mother warns the child or children of ways to avoid impending doom. In fact, some of the best stories deal with someone being alone or, in this case, having been left alone. At least the goats have their siblings, but they are actually more like a group of one entity as they face their fears. As Mother warns the children not to let anyone in the house while she is away, the children can answer in unison, "Yes, Mother," with some baaing.

When Mother prepares to leave the house, she can simply pantomime putting on her hat, putting on a coat, buttoning it, and getting her purse. The pantomiming of these objects rather than using real props or accessories encourages a child's imagination. Afterward, you can ask the child what color Mother's hat, coat, purse, and so on were. Was the coat long or short? What did her purse look like?

When Mother hugs her children goodbye, you can do a group hug. You can use an "air kiss," but you should stylize the hugs and kisses if you are in the role of a teacher or counselor to maintain necessary boundaries. A chair can be used as the door to establish placement. If it has an opening in the back like that in a folding chair, you can use that as the window.

The Wolf is the antagonist, the evil one. When initially portraying the Wolf during the storytelling portion, it helps to stylize him and make him one-dimensional and cartoonish. This gives him a comic flair and reduces his potential for being too frightening. A cartoonish Wolf with broad gestures is much less of a threat. You can have him tiptoe or slink toward the door to make him less realistic. He can lick his chops, rub his belly, and be overall "not too smart."

The Wolf arrives because he wants to devour the young kid goats. Some adults may be opposed to this idea, fearing it may scare the children or simply be too violent. Yet, psychologically, if a child faces such a tremendous situation, albeit through a fictional children's story, and can survive, it actually aids a child in facing life's difficulties that are hopefully not so life threatening but that nonetheless provoke fear. A child can face a difficult obstacle yet achieve success and have a happy ending.

It is very important that children be given a clear choice when they act out this particular story. Never force a child to act out a situation that he or she does not want to, no matter what the story calls for. If children are playing a goat that is to be either gobbled (again a stylized, less invasive term) by the Wolf or hide safely behind the grandfather clock, always give them the choice.

The children hear the knock on the door. You can have the Wolf knock in the air on an imaginary door and have someone else make the actual knocking sound on a hard surface from the side to make for an imaginary knocking while still using the chair to represent the door.

The children can answer in unison, "Who is it?" The Wolf needs to use a deep, gravelly voice when he responds. Again, when the Wolf clenches his fists and stomps his feet, he can do this in a nonthreatening, stylized, and broad manner, just like a two-year-old having a tantrum. This reduces his scariness and can add some distancing humor. Likewise, the Wolf should not lean toward the children if he is angry, for example, but lean back and away from the children to add distance. The children can also answer in a singsong manner when they reply, "Our mother doesn't have a voice like that." This also helps with memory.

Once the Wolf is turned away from the house by the young goats, he goes to a store. In the original story, he asks for chalk to eat, which in turn makes his voice soft like Mother's. In this newer version, he asks for honey to soften his voice, which seems like a wiser choice so that if children try this at home, they won't be tempted to eat chalk. When the Wolf meets the store clerk, there is ample room to add humor. The clerk can be overly scared and stammer and gesture wildly to make the story more exaggerated, and consequently safer and more distanced. As the Wolf drinks the honey, the child can add gulping sounds. The Wolf's voice dramatically softens after guzzling the honey. He throws the jar to the ground—again, this can be pantomimed. The Wolf can rub his belly and scratch under his armpits to make him seem cloddish.

Again, the Wolf goes back to the goats' house. As in many classic children's stories, you'll find repetition. Children tend to like repetition. It is comforting when a situation is replayed since the child gains more insight as to what might happen next. Repetition gives a child the chance to be "in the know."

During a scene such as this that the other children are not involved in, the children tend to watch like an audience and become absorbed in doing so. Some children will stay in character during the whole story, but others will stop and watch. Either is fine as long as they know not to be disruptive during other children's turns. Most children are good at being respectful of the other participants having their turn.

For the second time, the children keep the Wolf out of their house. The Wolf tries to trick them with his new, softer voice, but they see his dark paw and know that it is not their mother. The children have a false sense of outsmarting the Wolf. Again, when the Wolf goes to the baker, the dialogue can be improvised to add humor. You can use physicalization by having the baker jump in fear and hold the Wolf at arm's length, shaking in his shoes while handing him the flour. When the children are the Wolf, they have great fun "scaring" the clerk or baker. It can be a very funny scene when planned broadly. When the Wolf goes to the stores, it can be simply a few steps away in an upstage area.

The third time is the charm for the Wolf as he succeeds in tricking the goats into letting him into their house. It is quite a shock when the children are expecting Mother, only to find the Wolf at their doorstep. They say, "Mother is home!" and then run screaming in goat cries upon seeing the Wolf.

Children love repetition in stories. A pattern of reoccurring themes in threes is prevalent in classic children's stories. An example is when, in "The Three Little Pigs," the Wolf tries to blow down the houses three times. He succeeds twice, but the third time he is stumped and ultimately meets his demise. In "The Wolf and the Seven Kids," it is the third time that the pattern is broken and the Wolf gets into the house of the innocently waiting kid goats. The repetition builds suspense for the reader and, in this case, the young actors.

The emotions of this story are so far focused on a child's anxiety and fear of being left alone by Mother only to be tricked by an evil entity. It deals with mother-child trust versus a feeling of abandonment. Children who are exposed to this particular classic story can subconsciously examine their own innate feelings of what would happen in this worst-case scenario. Mother leaves, and a predator takes her place. For obvious reasons, the importance lies in the ending of the story to give the child a sense of security and well-being. So now that the Wolf has entered the Kids' home and safe dwelling, sheer horror ensues. You should predetermine before beginning the story where each child as a kid goat plans to hide.

The grandfather clock case is the only place where a kid goat is safe. Although the story states that only one goat hides in the grandfather clock, you must allow any child who chooses this option to be given this opportunity. Usually, most children prefer being safe in the clock and not eaten by the Wolf. Allow each child to make his own choice. Traditional casting methods are detrimental in this process. If all but one child select to be in the clock, then so be it. Usually, the adult can very readily become the grandfather clock, and the children who prefer to be safe can hide behind him. You can easily step in and out of the role of the clock as needed.

You should also predetermine which children are willing to be caught by the Wolf, who will be tagged and then simply curl up in a ball once tagged. Once the Wolf enters, you will find the children love to run and scream gleefully. As you narrate the story, you can improvise the hiding places based on the number of goats that you have and their preference for hiding places.

Again, keeping this scene stylized and cartoonish keeps it distanced and gamelike as the goats get "gobbled up." By keeping it playful and allowing each child to make his or her own choice in terms of role taking, the story remains safe. The children benefit from going through this pretend fear knowing that they will eventually be rescued. If you want to soften this scenario, you can have the Wolf put the goats in an imaginary sack or in the Wolf's pocket—whatever makes you feel more comfortable.

If you follow the original tale, the Wolf proceeds to tag the children and in a stylized manner gobble them up with a gulp. Pantomime or silent gesturing can be used for this moment. The licking of his chops adds to the broad and humorous nature of this plot twist. Any silence in the story adds a dramatic pause. This can be utilized effectively after the Wolf gobbles the goats, licks his lips, and rubs his belly in fullness, as if to suggest "What next?" Once the Wolf is full and content he leaves the house, leaving the door open. You can use a chair as the door or even a child in this part if he or she is so inclined.

As the Wolf leaves the house, he walks down to the edge of the lake and sits under a tall tree. Again, the adult can become the tree momentarily so that the Wolf can lie down beneath it, where he falls into a deep sleep. You can describe all stage directions within the narrative. For example, "Then the very full and now sleepy Wolf walked out to a tall tree and decided to lie down for a long rest. He yawned and stretched as he drifted off into dreamland." The children can literally act out all of the directions described in the narration in addition to adding their own ideas. A child's own ideas should always be encouraged. In encouraging children's imaginations, you should allow them to make the story their own, even if this means the story takes on a completely new life of its own to the point of being unrecognizable. In a one-on-one context, a child's ideas should be encouraged and utilized whenever possible, but with group work it is helpful to maintain the basic structure of the story in order to allow for a constant form. The context can waver slightly, but it is helpful to keep an outline for organization's sake when working with large numbers of children. You should remain flexible within the creative process while maintaining form.

As the Wolf sleeps under the tree, the kid goats that have been gobbled up can hide behind the tree while pretending to be in his belly. The sleeping Wolf with the hiding goats can be a very quiet scene. This is a nice contrast to the previous chaotic and climactic scene. Whenever a character is sleeping, you can use this as a control technique, which is particularly effective in group work. It can keep emotions from escalating, which can be paramount in acting out dramatic stories.

Just then, Mother comes home from the store. As soon as she sees the door ajar, she knows something is off, and she can literally stop in her tracks. Once she goes into the empty house and looks around, she calls to her children. There is a moment of silence, and then the clock strikes one, the cabinet opens, and the crying goats emerge. They tell Mother exactly what happened while she was gone. The wise and all-knowing universal mother has the children run to find a needle, thread, and scissors. The children do these things in pantomime. Then, quickly and quietly (which maintains order nicely), they go out in search of the Wolf and find the Wolf asleep.

Mother Goat snips open the Wolf's belly by pretending to snip through the air inches above the Wolf's actual belly. The kid goats pop out one by one. They can jump through the tree's trunk/legs for a fun effect. They jump up and down, excitedly shouting that they are okay. Once again, Mother must quiet them so that they don't wake the sleeping Wolf. Mother then sends her children to find "the biggest rocks they can find." Once again using pantomime, the children can carry very heavy rocks. One by one, the pantomime rocks are placed in the sleeping Wolf's belly. Then very quickly and accurately, Mother sews up the Wolf's belly, and the goat family runs back to the safety of their house, shuts the (chair) door, and locks it. If using an actual chair as the door, the children can peek through and around the chair as they watch the Wolf awaken.

The Wolf slowly wakes up as described in the story, thinking he has a belly full of goats. He doesn't know they were replaced with the heavy rocks. This is an instance when the children watching have a feeling of entitlement because they know something that the antagonist (Wolf) does not know. This allows the children to be one up on the Wolf! When the Wolf states, "I feel as if I ate rocks," this adds some comic relief to the story.

As the Wolf falls into the lake and meets his untimely demise, the child's world is now safe again. The Wolf's death is done in a stylized way as he tumbles head over heels, but it is important that the Wolf be destroyed so that security can ensue. Order is reestablished in the children's world. The obstacles were defeated in order to win. Happily ever after makes the bumpy ride and all the fear worthwhile. All is now restored to what is good. Announcing the story's title at the end of the story adds to the suspense and creates more of a punctuation.

It is survival of the fittest, exemplified in this case by the drive and determination of the Mother combined with the courage of the youngest protagonists. Children love this story for all of its subliminal meaning, but more because they can outsmart the antagonist after experiencing some scary moments in the making. It is not only a significant classic children's fairy tale but also a lot of fun to play act because of its life-threatening moments that result in life saving and reaffirming feelings of security.

The playful qualities that are added with the "peek-a-boo" nature of "Who is at the door?" combined with the "tag game" when the Wolf attacks are important in balancing the otherwise serious life conflicts.

Tips

- Use as many or as few kid goats as your group and the preferences of your group allow.

- As the story begins, the kid goats are sleeping, which children love to pretend, plus this keeps great control of the group.

- Creativity and imagination often need boundaries to maintain the newly found energy.

- As the goats sleep, they can snore or be dreaming.

- Child goats can slowly awaken and pretend to yawn and stretch.

- Mother Goat can be centered in an actual chair for positioning, and all of the goat children can gather around her.

- As Mother Goat feeds the children, they pretend to eat and can ask for and receive more food.

- A goat language can be created by interjecting baas into the English dialogue on a periodic basis.

- The animals in this story are all humanized, so they can walk and talk. The young goats can walk on all fours, but Mother may choose to walk upright.

- If a child chooses not to use words for any reason, he or she should be made to feel comfortable by using just the animal sounds.

- Children playing a group of animals can talk in unison, which helps them to remember the words as they can cue or be cued by their neighbor.

- If more than one child wants to be the Mother, then one can have Moms in the story.

- You can use a chair to represent the door.

- When initially telling or sharing the story, it is helpful to present the Wolf in a stylized or cartoonish manner, using broad gestures and tiptoeing, for example, rather than attempting a realistic portrayal.

- The Wolf can knock in the air on the imaginary door (even when using a chair), and another child can be selected to make the actual knocking noise on any hard surface.

- The kid goats can answer the Wolf's knocking by saying in unison, "Who is it?"

- The Wolf uses a deep, gravelly voice when he first speaks to the young goats.

- When the Wolf gets upset, it should be done like a two-year-old's temper tantrum to create some humor and reduce any threat.

- There is plenty of room for humor when the store clerk is suddenly surprised by the Wolf's visit. The clerk can stammer and exaggerate his gestures.

- The Wolf can add gulping sounds as he guzzles the honey. Then the Wolf switches to a soft and sweet voice like Mother's.

- The child playing the role of the Wolf can have fun sneaking up and scaring the baker.

- There's no need to use real flour when acting out this scene. Although it would be fun to use talcum powder, pantomime is fine.

- As the Wolf finally tricks his way into the goats' house, the kids scatter and hide.

- If a child hides behind the grandfather clock (usually played by the leader), he is safe from the Wolf.

- Any kid goat who doesn't hide behind the clock will be tagged by the Wolf as in a tag game, and this represents being gobbled up.

- More than one child can choose to be safe behind the grandfather clock. As many as want to can hide there.

- If a kid goat is caught or tagged by the Wolf, he or she can roll up in a ball shape.

- As the Wolf gobbles up the goats, he can lick his lips and rub his belly.

- If a child doesn't elect to be the tree, the leader can easily step into the role while continuing to narrate the story.

- The Wolf sleeps in front of the tree, and the "gobbled" goats line up behind the tree in a squatting or sitting position and hide quietly.

- As the leader narrates the story, he/she can describe all of the specific stage directions for the young actors to follow.

- Whoever is playing the role of the grandfather clock can make the chiming noise as the clock strikes one.

- Once Mother and the "safe" kids find the sleeping Wolf, Mother Goat pretends to snip open the Wolf's belly without actually touching the Wolf at all.

- The goat children can pretend to jump out of the Wolf's belly one by one.

- Then, very quietly, so as not to awaken the Wolf, all of the goats run off to find large pantomimed rocks.

- Once the Wolf's belly is full of rocks and air-sewn back up, the goat family runs back home to safety.

- The goat family can peek through or around the chair that is being used to represent the door.

- The Wolf leans over for a drink of water from the lake and tumbles into the deep blue due to the weight of the rocks in his belly.

- A child or children can pretend to be the lake, which devours the Wolf entirely.

- A celebration cheer or song always allows for a good sense of closure for the goat family.

Table 2.1. Summary of Story Elements

	"The Wolf and the Seven Kids"
Characters	Mother, Seven Kid Goats, Wolf, Store Clerk, Baker
Inanimate Roles	Tree, lake
Location	Goats' house, store, bakery, big lake
Timeline	Long ago and far away
Difficulty	Complex
Length	Long
Props	Blue material for lake
Costumes	Goat ears and tails, bell necklaces, goatees, wolf ears and tail, baker's apron and hat, clerk attire
Set	Tree, lake
Theme	Don't be tricked by a clever wolf when Mother is away
Plot	Repetitious
Emotion	High—life-threatening
Conflict Resolution	Resolution due to Mother's swift thinking
Pace	Steady, frantic, joyous
Moral	Don't let the wolf/stranger trick you—follow your instincts

"The Wolf and the Seven Kids" is so innately dramatic that children absolutely love to play act this tale. This fairy tale is actually filled with suspense and keeps the young actors on the edge of their seats. They will scream with glee when the Wolf chases them, just as in a game of tag. This is markedly contrasted with the scene where they hide in the Wolf's belly, waiting to pop out like popcorn! "The Wolf and the Seven Kids" has always been one of children's favorite stories to dramatize. The next story, "The Gingerbread Man," is all about the chase.

Note

1. Jacob Ludwig Carl Grimm and Wilhelm Carl Grimm, *Grimms' Fairy Tales: Forty-two Household Tales* (Charleston, SC: Forgotten Books, 2008).

CHAPTER THREE
THE GINGERBREAD MAN

The story "The Gingerbread Man" is also known as "The Gingerbread Boy."[1] The first written appearance was in May 1875 in the *St. Nicholas Magazine*, a popular magazine for children in the nineteenth century. It was published but with no author. Although this was the first printing, "The Gingerbread Man" was already a very well-known tale. There are several renditions of "The Gingerbread Man" still in print today.

"The Gingerbread Man" is all about the chase. It is a very high-energy and footloose story. I will describe some specific techniques to keep the fun under control. The Gingerbread Cookie is essentially running for his life, yet taunting and teasing all along the way. The Gingerbread Man is quite mischievous and therefore great fun to play act.

And even though the horse could gallop, she just could not catch the Gingerbread Man.

The Story

A long time ago, and very far away, there lived an old woman and an old man. One day, the old woman was fixing lunch for the old man while he was working in the yard. As she fixed his lunch, she decided to make him a special treat, one of her husband's favorites.

She took a big bowl and added lots of nice ingredients. She added some flour, some sugar, and some surprises, too. She mixed and stirred. She stirred and mixed until she formed a dough ball. Then the old woman rolled out the dough until it was just right. She cut out the shape. She took some raisins and made some buttons. She took some chocolate chips for eyes. Then the old woman made a licorice smile.

She made a beautiful gingerbread cookie, which she then placed in the oven. And on went the timer. The old woman called to the old man, "Old man, time for lunch. Come in, old man."

The old man came in from working in the yard, and he was scratching and sniffing. "Woman, where is my lunch?" he grumbled.

"Here you are, old man, a nice sandwich and some lemonade." The old woman gave her husband his lunch and then said, "Old man, guess what I've made for you." She paused. "One of your favorites. One of your favorite desserts."

"Is it cherry pie?" he asked.

"No," she said.

"Is it chocolate cake?" he pleaded.

"No," she said.

"Umm, banana cream pie?"

"No," she replied. "Gingerbread men!"

"Ohh!" he cried. "Yummy! I can't wait!"

Just then the timer rang, and as the old woman opened the oven door, much to her surprise, the gingerbread cookie jumped out of the oven!

"Oh, my stars!" cried the old woman.

"Run, run, as fast as you can, you can't catch me, I'm the Gingerbread Man!"

And with that, the gingerbread cookie ran out the door.

"Hey! Wait!" called the old man. "Come back here!"

"Stop, cookie, stop!" called the old woman. Then the old woman and the old man started to chase after the cookie. But since they were so old, they just couldn't go very fast. The gingerbread cookie was long gone. He ran away.

The gingerbread cookie ran on and on until he came to a cow. The cow looked at him and said, "Mooooo, I would like to eat you with some mmmmmmilk!"

"Run, run, as fast as you can, you can't catch me, I'm the Gingerbread Man!"

And off he ran. Well, the cow ran after the cookie, but the cookie was just too fast.

Next, the Gingerbread Man came up to a horse. "Neeee-igh!" said the horse. "I would like to eat you."

"I have run from an old woman. I have run from an old man. I have run from a cow. Run, run, as fast as you can, you can't catch me, I'm the Gingerbread Man!"

"Oh, yes I can!" said the horse.

But the Gingerbread Man was so fast, he quickly ran away, and even though the horse could gallop, he could not catch the Gingerbread Man.

"Run, run, as fast as you can, you can't catch me, I'm the Gingerbread Man!" cried out the cookie in glee.

Off ran the Gingerbread Man, through the fields and over the dales. He ran and ran until he came up to two men working in the fields. It was a hot day, and they were working very hard. In fact, they were working up a hunger. When they saw the Gingerbread Man, they said, "Hey, you, stop! We are going to eat you up!"

"Run, run, as fast as you can, you can't catch me, I'm the Gingerbread Man!" shouted the cookie, as he ran away.

"We're going to catch you!" shouted the two workmen.

Just then, the two workmen, and the old man, and the old woman, and the cow, and the horse came running to catch the Gingerbread Man. As he looked over his shoulder, the Gingerbread Man saw them all shouting and yelling at him to stop.

"Come back here, you cookie, you!"

"Stop! You can't get away!"

"We're going to eat you!" they all shouted.

Well, the cookie came to a wide river, and the crowd was getting closer and closer. About that time, a fox appeared by the riverbank. "I can help you, my friend," said the fox slyly. "Just jump on my back, and I will swim you across to safety."

"No!" said the Gingerbread Man. "I don't trust you. I won't do it!"

But the old man, the old woman, the horse, the cow, and the workmen were all getting closer still.

"You can trust me," said the fox. "I won't hurt you, I promise."

So the cookie, who didn't know what to do, finally agreed to jump onto the fox's back. And the fox began to swim across the river. But the Gingerbread Man's foot began to get wet.

"My foot is getting wet! What should I do?" cried the Gingerbread Man.

"Jump on my shoulders," said the fox.

So the Gingerbread Man jumped onto the fox's shoulders. They continued across the river. But the Gingerbread Man's feet began to get wet again.

"My foot is getting wet! What should I do?" cried the Gingerbread Man.

"Jump on my head," said the fox.

So the Gingerbread Man jumped onto the fox's head. "Oh, thank you. Yes, that is much better," said the Gingerbread Man.

But then the water began to get even higher.

"Uh oh! The river is rising and my feet are getting wet again! Help!" cried the cookie.

"Jump on my nose," said the fox.

And the Gingerbread Man did just that. He jumped onto the fox's nose. Then, suddenly, "Gulp!" said the fox.

The fox gobbled up the Gingerbread Man in one bite, and the cookie was no more. The fox licked his lips.

And that is the story of "The Gingerbread Man."

"Climb on my back; I won't hurt you," said the fox.

Questions

- What are some ingredients that the old woman can add to the big bowl?

- As the old woman stirs the dough in the bowl, can the pre-formed cookie roll about?

- When the old woman adds the decorations for the face, can the cookie react with new eyes and smile? (Example: From closed eyes to open eyes, and from neutral face to a smile.)

- As the old woman cuts the cookie shape, can the cookie spring into form?

- How grumbly is the old man?

- What was he doing in the yard?

- Can the old man pretend to eat his lunch using pantomime?

- Who can ding like the oven timer?

- How does the Gingerbread Man stand? Stiff like a cookie?

- What does the old woman think when she sees the Gingerbread Man jump out of the oven?

- What does the old man think when he hears the Gingerbread Man taunt them?

- Who can run faster, the old man and woman or the Gingerbread Man?

- How fast can the Gingerbread Man run?

- How does a cow sound?

- How does a cow chew its cud?

- Who ran faster, the cow or the Gingerbread Man?

- How does a horse sound?

- What does the horse want to do to the Gingerbread Man?

- How does a horse run?

- Who ran faster, the horse or the Gingerbread Man?

- Let's see how the workmen are working. Are they raking or shoveling?

- How hungry are the workmen?

- Can the workmen catch the Gingerbread Man?

- If you are a river, how would you move?

- Is the fox sneaky?

- How does the fox move? How does he move in the water?

- Does the Gingerbread Man want to go with the fox at first?

- How do we pretend that the Gingerbread Man is climbing up the fox's back?

- Why does the Gingerbread Man change his mind and jump onto the fox's back?

- Can the river splash up onto the Gingerbread Man's feet?

- How do we pretend that the fox ate the Gingerbread Man?

- Was the fox to be trusted?

Exploration

"The Gingerbread Man" lends itself to dramatization for many reasons. The main character is a cookie. The Gingerbread Cookie has human qualities although it is an inanimate object. Children enjoy being the Gingerbread Man because he is loved by everyone he meets, albeit because they yearn to devour him. More importantly, he taunts the antagonists in the story, and they constantly chase him. Children love to be given permission to run within a story, especially while indoors. Therefore, this story has high intensity in terms of physical action.

As the story begins, we find the old woman baking the Old Man's favorite dessert—a gingerbread cookie. The process of mixing the dough with all of the necessary ingredients is a fun yet challenging piece to enact. The child can be mixed and stirred in an imaginary bowl with an imaginary spoon. The Gingerbread Man can tumble and roll about as he or she becomes the cookie dough. Then, the old woman rolls out the dough (child) with the imaginary rolling pin. The child playing the role of the cookie then flattens out with no actual physical contact necessary. The old woman simply "air-rolls" the dough. Then, again without any physical contact, the old woman proceeds to decorate the cookie after she has cut out the cookie shape. She can use raisins, chocolate chips, licorice, or frosting (all to be pantomimed). As the woman decorates the cookie's face, the child opens his eyes and smiles with the newly formed mouth. Then, into the pantomimed oven goes the cookie to bake.

The old man enters and has lunch. A guessing game ensues as he tries to guess what is baking in the oven. A guessing game adds fun and suspense to the story since the children all know what is baking, but the old man gives the illusion of not knowing. The cookie baking in the oven has been equated to childbirth. Once the cookie is "born," he developmentally skips the crawling stage. He is born to run immediately!

The cookie takes delight in being chased, as will the child playing this role. A boy does not have to play the part of the Gingerbread Man. If a girl plays the part of the Gingerbread Man, she can be the Gingerbread Girl, or, if more than one child is playing this role, they can be the Gingerbread Kids. It could even simply be the Gingerbread Cookie, which is not gender specific.

So, the chase begins with the old man and the old woman running after the cookie. It is up to you, the narrator, as to how much freedom to give the young actors in this chase scene. If you feel the need to maintain some control, slow-motion running can be utilized. If the children do actually run, use a "freeze" technique to stop them on cue. By calling out "Freeze," the structure of the story is maintained. Also, running in place is an effective technique to use within this dramatization.

The young protagonist is trying to gain mastery of his destiny while running haphazardly among a society waiting to devour him should he slip. As the cookie runs, he is exerting energy. The ongoing theme of the antagonists is one of hunger. The Gingerbread Man is, therefore, running for his life. There is a certain urgency in the chase scenes. They can be played out like a game of tag; however, the Gingerbread Man is never tagged. Adding a game such as tag to the story makes it all the more play-ful for children to act out.

The character of the Gingerbread Man is mischievous, defiant, agile, and fast. This role can be very engaging for children as they are given per-mission to act naughty within the safety and confines of the story. What child doesn't want to be "bad"? It is healthy for a child to try on this role, and it will not perpetuate misbehaving outside of the story but rather al-low a child to explore various perspectives through play.

In this particular version of the story, the Gingerbread Man is chased by the old man and old woman, and then by a cow, a horse, and finally, two workmen. Children often like to play the roles of animals. When working with a group of children, more than one child can play a par-ticular animal, according to his preference. So you could have a herd of cattle or several horses. New animals can easily be added to the story, such as a cat, a bear, a jaguar, and so on. The choices are limited only by the child's imagination. The story is repetitive, which is comforting to young children, as they know exactly what will happen next.

After the story is first shared with the children, and once the children have selected the specific role they would like to become, a few minutes can be spent practicing their parts. This can easily be done before the group enacts the whole story. The character of the horse can have gal-loping or prancing movements and a neighing sound. Let the children practice moving and sounding like a horse. The character of the cow can chew its cud as the jaw moves from side to side. The children can practice mooing. The instructor can create a simple hand gesture similar to that of an orchestra leader to stop the animal sounds on cue and maintain control as needed.

The two hungry workmen may be presented as bumbling fools to add some comic relief. They could be presented as buffoons, which makes the cookie appear to be all the smarter in comparison. Children love the low-est form of comedy—slapstick. Any slipping on banana peels or getting stuck in the mud during the chase scene can be fun for them. The children may have original ideas if you choose to add comic relief to the story.

The last scene of this story is the most memorable. The fox is a trickster. The fox in this tale is cunning and witty. The role of the fox is one of deceit as he or she cannot be trusted. The fox is quite fearless and goes where others dare not go. The character of the fox is one of the only antagonists in a fairy tale that wins in the end. The sly fox is calculating, and he ultimately survives. The fox will not be defeated. Children are drawn to this role for these very reasons. They want to win at all costs, no matter what it may take. It is a fun role for many to enact.

The Gingerbread Man is being chased by everyone he has met thus far in the story when he comes to the river and meets the fox. The Gingerbread Man can't cross the river by himself or he will dissolve. As he looks over his shoulder, he sees the group of angry people and animals coming for him. The young actors can run in place and shake their fists as they yell for the cookie to stop. The conflict arises as to what the cookie should now do. He feels stuck for a minute. Then, the fox makes the cookie an offer to help him across the river by having him jump onto the fox's back. The cookie hesitates momentarily but feels he has no choice but to trust the fox.

The river can be played by any child or children who choose to become the rapidly moving water. The children playing the water gradually rise up the poor cookie as he scrambles to higher and dryer ground. The cookie is first on the fox's back, then shoulders, then head, and then nose, and after that is gobbled up. A lip-smacking gulp is heard from the fox as he gobbles up the cookie! To act out this scene, the cookie can place his hands on the fox's back, shoulders, head, and nose if the child playing the Gingerbread Man is too heavy to climb onto the fox's back. The child playing the cookie could also just jump alongside the Fox and simply pretend to climb higher and higher. Once the cookie is gobbled, the actor can curl up in a ball and roll down the river into crumbs. A blue cloth can also be used as the river, using a waving motion to create a ripple effect.

Sometimes the child playing the Gingerbread Man decides that he or she doesn't want to be gobbled up in the end. Never insist on it. Simply see whether someone else wants to step in and be gobbled up for fun. Keep it light. Or, if everyone agrees, you could change the ending, although the Gingerbread Man, after all, is just a cookie.

Tips

- Some children love to be a mischievous cookie.

- The Gingerbread Man can be played by a boy or a girl and be referred to as the Gingerbread Cookie.

- Children in general love this story because it involves chasing, and children love to run.

- This story is a high-intensity story because of the physical action.

- The making of the cookie is a fun yet challenging process.

- A child can be mixed and gently rolled around with an imaginary spoon in an imaginary bowl by the old woman.

- The child playing the part of the cookie can then be rolled out flat with a pretend rolling pin.

- As the old woman adds the decorations to the cookie, he opens his eyes and smiles.

- As the cookie bakes, the old man plays a guessing game with his wife to determine what is baking in the oven.

- Once the cookie comes to life, the chase begins. But the old Man and woman run too slowly to catch him.

- The characters can run in place if space is limited or run in slow motion if the leader deems it necessary to control the excitement.

- Use a "freeze" technique by calling out "Freeze" if the leader ever needs to maintain control of the creativity.

- Those chasing the cookie can never catch him and must resist the temptation.

- The horse or cow in the story can be played by a few children each, numbers permitting, resulting in herds.

- The two workmen cannot outsmart or even catch the cookie.

- The fox is cunning and much like the wolf in other popular fairy tales, although the fox will achieve his goal.

- The cookie can simply put his hand on the fox's back, shoulders, head, and nose to represent climbing on the fox.

- Children can become the river, which plays an active role in splashing up on the Gingerbread Man, forcing him to climb higher on the fox.

- The fox can practice making a lip-smacking gulp, and the Gingerbread Man can roll into a ball and be swept away down the river.

Table 3.1.   Summary of Story Elements

	"The Gingerbread Man"
Characters	Old woman, old man, Gingerbread Cookie, cow, horse, two men, fox
Inanimate Roles	River, oven
Location	A country house, fields
Timeline	Long ago and not too far away
Difficulty	Moderate
Length	Medium
Props	n/a
Costumes	Apron, three hats, vest, cow ears and tail, horse ears and tail, fox ears and tail
Set	Oven, river
Theme	Run, run as fast as you can
Plot	Repetition—I will eat you, run, repeat
Emotions	Frantic, taunting, escaping
Conflict Resolution	Fox eats, resolution ends badly for cookie, but he is a cookie after all
Pace	Very fast
Moral	Don't trust a fox; running as fast as you can = danger

The story of "The Gingerbread Man" is fun and frivolous. Children will find themselves in a cookie's world, complete with one-dimensional characters and one chase scene after another. Because of the chasing and impending doom for the protagonist, the story is very high energy for children to perform. The next tale, "Little Red Riding Hood," also includes gobbling up on the part of the antagonist, but, luckily, Little Red Riding Hood and her grandmother fare better than the Gingerbread Man.

Note

1. "The Gingerbread Boy," *St. Nicholas Magazine*, May 1875.

CHAPTER FOUR
LITTLE RED RIDING HOOD

"Little Red Riding Hood"[1] dates as far back as the ninth century. This captivating story was originally an oral tale told as a bedtime story and around campfires. The first published version was written by Charles Perrault in his first book, titled *Tales from the Past, with Morals: Tales of Mother Goose*. Perrault's first book was published in 1697, when he was sixty-nine years old. Since the story's first publication, "Little Red Riding Hood" has been adapted into several books, plays, and movies, including the Brothers Grimm's 1812 publication. As with many classic fairy tales, the protagonist of the story is Little Red Riding Hood, the title character of the story. The antagonist is the Wolf, who interacts with Little Red Riding Hood in the infamous "My, Grandmother, what big ears you have" scene. "Little Red Riding Hood" is one of the oldest and best-known fairy tales.

The story of "Little Red Riding Hood" is so well known that it is a wonderful choice for dramatization. When a story is already familiar to a child, it makes for a better foundation upon which to build. The characters, story line, and infamous dialogue make for a perfect springboard for the child acting. It is a wonderful choice for children to enact, complete with a tricky wolf who almost wins, but not quite.

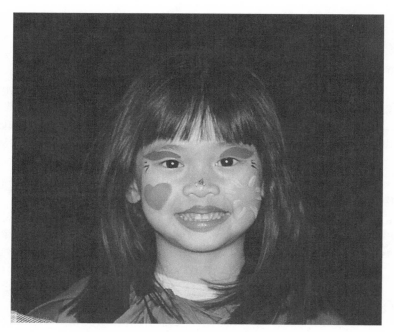

"Grandmother," said Little Red, "what big eyes you have!"

The Story

A long time ago and very far away, there lived a little girl and her mother. The little girl's name was Little Red Riding Hood.

One morning, her mother said, "Little Red, Little Red! I need you to go and visit Grandmother. She is quite sick today, so I fixed a basket of goodies for you to take to her."

"Yes, Mother, I'll take this basket of goodies to Grandmother. I sure hope she feels better soon!"

And then Mother said, "Now remember, Little Red, don't talk to strangers. Just go straight along the path to Grandmother's, and that's it."

"Yes, Mother, I won't talk to strangers. Don't worry about me! Can't wait to see Grandmother!"

And with that, Little Red took the basket of goodies and skipped through the woods, tra la la, tra la la along the way, until suddenly, a big, sneaky Wolf jumped out from behind the tree and said, "Ah, little girl, what do you have in the basket?"

"Oh!" said Little Red. "I just have some goodies for my grandmother. She's not feeling well."

"Oh," said the Wolf, "your grandmother's not feeling well. That's a shame. And where did you say your grandmother lives?"

"Oh," said Little Red, "Grandmother lives two trees down to the right, turn left along the stream, across the path and then it's nestled in the woods right there. Why do you ask?"

"No reason," said the Wolf. "I just hope your grandmother feels better soon. I must go." And with that, the Wolf was gone.

"Hmm," said Little Red. "Imagine that. Oh, well. I'm on my way. And I'm not going to talk to any strangers, just like Mother said."

And Little Red skipped along, through the woods, tra la la, tra la la, just like that, along the path to Grandmother's house. Well, what she didn't know was that the mean old sneaky Wolf took a shortcut and got to Grandmother's house before Little Red did. He knocked on the door.

Grandmother said, "Who is it?"

"It's Little Red!" said the Wolf, pretending to sound sweet like Little Red.

"Oh, come in, come in, darling. I can't wait to see you!"

But the sneaky Wolf came in through the house, and Grandmother said, "Ahh! You're not Little Red, you're the Wolf!"

And the Wolf gobbled up Grandmother in one big bite.

He took Grandmother's nightgown, put it on, and crawled into Grandmother's bed to wait for Little Red. Just then, Little Red came up to the front door. Tap, tap, tap. Tap, tap, tap.

"Who is it?" said the Wolf.

"It's Little Red, Grandmother!"

"Come in, dear," said the Wolf, pretending to be Grandmother.

And Little Red went into the house with the basket of goodies. "Grandmother, Grandmother, I brought you a basket of goodies. I hope you're feeling better."

"Oh, yes, dear, I'm feeling much better," said the Wolf.

"Grandmother," said Little Red, "What big eyes you have."

"The better to see you with, my dear."

"Grandmother, what big ears you have."

"The better to hear you with, my dear."

"Grandmother, what big teeth you have."

"The better to gobble you up with!" said the Wolf. And he leaped out of Grandmother's bed.

Little Red screamed, "Aaaaah!"

And the Wolf gobbled up Little Red!

Well, just about that time, there happened to be a Woodsman out chopping down some trees with his ax, and he heard Little Red's cries. "Somebody needs help!" said the Woodsman. So he ran over to Grandmother's house, and he saw the Wolf with a big belly filled with Grandmother and Little Red.

Chop, chop, chop, went the Woodsman. Chop, chop, chop. And Grandmother and Little Red popped right out of the Big

Bad Wolf's belly. They were just fine. They looked as good as new!

"Phew," said the Grandmother, "what happened?"

"Oh, thank you," said Little Red to the Woodsman, "thank you so much! We really appreciate you stepping in and saving us. We really do."

And do you know that that Big Bad Wolf never bothered anybody ever again?

And that's the story of "Little Red Riding Hood."

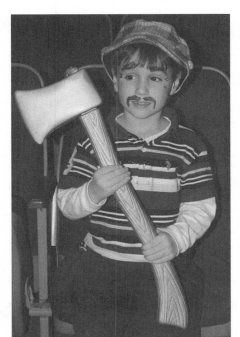

Just about that time, there happened to be a Woodsman nearby chopping down some trees.

Questions

- How did Little Red Riding Hood get her name?

- With what is Grandmother sick?

- What is in the basket?

- What does Mother warn Little Red about?

- Can you skip like Little Red?

- Where did the Wolf come from?

- How does a sneaky Wolf move?

- How can you pretend to be old like Grandmother?

- How can we make a bed?

- How does the Wolf change his voice to sound like Little Red?

- How does Grandmother feel when she sees the Wolf?

- How can we pretend that the Wolf gobbles up Grandmother?

- How does the Wolf change his voice to sound like Grandmother?

- Can you make your eyes big like the Wolf's?

- How can Little Red pretend not to see the Wolf when she is looking right at him?

- Can you make your ears big like the Wolf's?

- How big are the Wolf's teeth?

- At what point does Little Red know that it is a Wolf?

- How loudly does Little Red yell when the Wolf jumps out of bed?

- How do we pretend that the Wolf gobbles up Little Red?

- How can the Woodsman pretend to chop open the Wolf's belly?

- Let me see Grandmother and Little Red pretend to pop out of the Wolf's belly.

- How are Grandmother and Little Red doing?

- How can they thank the Woodsman for saving their lives?

- What happens to the Wolf?

- Do they live happily ever after?

Exploration

"Little Red Riding Hood" is a timeless and universal tale. It is well known around the world and has a compact cast of unforgettable characters. "Little Red Riding Hood" is a relatively easy story for children to act out, in part due to its familiarity.

This classic fairy tale takes place long ago and very far away, which gives the needed distance to the reader or, in the case of dramatizations, the players or viewers. In a world where wolves can gobble someone up, it is best to put much time and distance between the child and the action of this imaginary tale. It is also recommended to use the original version of the story, as opposed to the more recent, watered-down version. "Little Red Riding Hood" lends itself to dramatization very readily, as it is a short tale with some famous scenes to enact.

As this cautionary tale begins, we meet Mother and her daughter, our protagonist, Little Red Riding Hood. The presenting conflict or problem is that Grandmother is sick. Mother asks Little Red to take a basket of goodies to Grandmother. At this point, Mother warns her not to talk to strangers. This foreshadows what is about to happen. As Little Red Riding Hood skips through the forest, out jumps the sneaky Wolf from behind the imaginary trees. If working with a group of children, the boys and girls can easily become the trees of the forest in an ensemble fashion.

Little Red is naïve, and the Wolf is tricky. As they converse, the plot thickens now that the Wolf discovers where Grandmother lives. The story unfolds as the Wolf takes a shortcut to Grandmother's house and gobbles her up. You should present the Wolf in a stylized fashion. A one-dimensional and cartoonish Wolf is more pleasing to children, as opposed to a realistic-acting Wolf. A stylized Wolf is more distanced and therefore less threatening than a realistic carnivore.

When the Wolf "gobbles up" Grandmother, it should be done in a playful way, as in a game of tag. The Wolf can tag the person and then pretend to gobble her up, complete with the punctuating gulp and tummy rub.

So the Big Bad Wolf is now lying in Grandmother's bed, awaiting Little Red Riding Hood's arrival. Little Red is sweet, young, and an easy target. As she skips through the woods, she has no idea of what lies ahead. In fact, Little Red is loved universally, in part because she is so trusting.

Ironically, there is something innately likable about the Big Bad Wolf, or he would not have any control over us. Children love to play him. You can conceivably have a whole pack of wolves when enacting the story because more than one child may want to play this enticing part. Notice that the Wolf's own hunger will ultimately seal his fate. His greed will get the better of him in the end. The character of the Wolf is the antagonist of the story. He is barbaric with a bestial appetite. The Big Bad Wolf is a threat to anyone he meets in this story. Subconsciously, he taps into our devouring drives, yet on an antisocial level. Children love to be given permission to pretend to be bad and bestial, if only for a few minutes, and if only through their play.

Once Little Red arrives at Grandmother's house and enters her room, the infamous scene begins. "Grandmother, what big eyes . . . ears . . . teeth you have," says Little Red. The physical senses are unleashed. The reader or audience knows what the Wolf has done, disguised in Grandmother's nightgown, and they know exactly what he is about to do. As in the original tale, the Wolf jumps out of bed and gobbles up Little Red, just as she calls out for help. In newer versions of this classic, Little Red gets stuffed in the closet with Grandmother, but children don't require this watered-down version. They may not choose to be in the role of the gobbled-up character, which they should never be forced to do. However, the characters can't go through such a disaster and survive if they haven't been devoured.

The Woodsman, who happens to hear Little Red's cries, comes to her rescue by chopping open the Wolf's belly so that Little Red and Grandmother can jump out unscathed. Although we don't want to portray Little Red as helpless and in need of a Woodsman to save her, this is how the story has been told for generations. Some children will enjoy being the

Woodsman and stepping in to "save the day." The Woodsman is a hero and can be played by a boy or a girl. The Woodsman should not actually chop the Wolf's belly with force, but pretend to do an "air chop." Little Red and Grandmother can be hiding behind the Wolf and jump out upon hearing the chopping. The Wolf can fall down dead in a slow-motion and stylized manner. The remaining characters all rejoice. A song and dance of celebration can ensue. Woodland creatures can join in the festivities, a happy ending for all except the Big Bad Wolf, who, after all, got what he deserved.

The best part of this story is its familiarity. Because it is known throughout the world, it lends itself very readily to dramatization. Children like to play act a story that they have heard over and over again. In fact, they often like to enact a story that they know, taking on a different role or, at times, keeping the same part. The child's preference should always be permitted. The child will tell you whom he wants to become, and this should always be honored.

If no one wants to play Grandmother, for example, which is sometimes the case in the offering of an elderly role, then you should step into that role. If several children choose to be the Wolf, you may choose to become a wolf with the "pack" just long enough to encourage movement and dialogue as needed. You should feel free to step in and out of the story as needed by becoming the narrator and then even a tree as deemed necessary for a significant moment. For example, when the Wolf is hiding and spying on Little Red in the forest, he can be hiding behind you as the tree. This would be applicable if a child does not want the part of the tree. For this tale of Little Red Riding Hood, an ensemble of children could easily become a chorus by taking on the evolving roles of trees, woodland creatures, and Grandmother's cottage.

With such a classic story, you need to keep the characters as close to the original as possible. The fun of the story is in the one-dimensionality of the cartoon characters that makes them easy to play. Also, with such a traditional story, you need to keep the plot as true to the original as possible. You want to encourage the children to brainstorm and create their own ideas within the set structure of the predetermined story line. For example, one child might say, "I want to be a mommy wolf."

"Yes, this is a fine idea. How would Mommy Wolf walk? What would Mommy Wolf say?"

Or one child might say, "I want to be Little Pink Riding Hood."

"Yes, a great idea! Little Red will be Little Pink. And what can she wear?"

Or "I want to be Little Red's father as the story begins."

You can use all of these creative ideas while shaping them within the confines of the plot.

Always try to utilize the children's ideas whenever applicable, and use questioning to encourage your child's use of imagination. Children can become the inanimate objects as well. Someone may volunteer to be the Woodsman's ax, and this would be a fun idea to act out. "Are you sharp or dull? Can you make a chopping sound?"

This story is relatively short, with approximately three primary scenes, so it is easily doable within any time constraints.

Tips

- Acting out "Little Red Riding Hood" is easier than some other stories because it is so familiar to children.

- Be sure to include "long ago and far away" when starting the story to establish much-needed distance for the children.

- You can use an actual basket or simply pantomime the use of a basket.

- Have Mother warn Little Red, as this foreshadows what is to come in the tale.

- Children can become the forest, complete with sounds, if you are working with a group.

- The Wolf is tricky and sneaky in thought and action.

- It is helpful to make the Wolf cartoonish and stylized, rather than realistic, to lessen the fear factor when working with very young children.

- Little Red Riding Hood is not particularly scared of the Wolf when she first meets him because the Wolf disarms her with his smooth style.

- Use a playful game of tag when the Wolf gobbles up Grandmother. When the Wolf tags you, you have been gobbled. You then must hide behind someone or something.

- Some children like to play the sweet, naïve, and unknowing Little Red Riding Hood. The Big Bad Wolf with all of his wickedness is a great character and can therefore be quite appealing for others to play.

- If a child wants to be the Big Bad Wolf, it will not make him or her mean like the Wolf in everyday life; it is only a playful and permitted way to explore being the bad guy.

- The scene with Little Red Riding Hood and the Wolf in bed disguised as Grandmother is an infamous one. Children love to play out this scene because they know it and it is familiar to them.

- The repetition of the questioning, "What big eyes you have, what big ears you have, what big teeth you have," is comforting to children and also builds up the suspense to the point where the Wolf pounces on Little Red Riding Hood.

- If children are too squeamish regarding the gobbling up of Grandmother and Little Red, they can be given the option of being stuffed into the closet instead.

- Some children like to pretend to be gobbled up as long as they are eventually freed. Others do not want to be gobbled. Do not force them.

- Little Red Riding Hood can let out a cry for help just before being caught by the Wolf. If you are in a school setting, she will need to keep her voice down a bit. She could use a whisper shout.

- The Woodsman saves the day when he hears Little Red Riding Hood's cries. He should stop what he is doing and run in to help as fast as he can. Children love to be given permission to run, especially indoors.

- The ax can be pantomimed; just use an air-chopping motion to the Wolf's belly.

- Little Red Riding Hood and Grandmother pop out of the Wolf's belly unscathed as the Wolf collapses to the floor.

- It is important when dramatizing a classic children's story to stay true to the characters as described and to the story line. Contemporizing fairy tales is not necessary.

Table 4.1.   Summary of Story Elements

	"Little Red Riding Hood"
Characters	Mother, Little Red Riding Hood, Wolf, Grandmother, Woodsman
Inanimate Roles	Woods
Location	Mother's house, woods, Grandmother's house
Timeline	Long ago and far away
Difficulty	Simple
Length	Short to moderate
Props	Basket, blanket
Costumes	Red hooded cape, apron, wolf ears and tail, granny gown and cap
Set	Woods, houses, bed
Theme	Never trust a stranger
Plot	Leaving home, trusting Wolf, Wolf's deceit of Grandmother and Little Red Riding Hood
Emotion	Gobbling, high
Conflict Resolution	Story is resolved—happy ending
Pace	Roller coaster
Moral	Don't trust strangers

The classic "Little Red Riding Hood" is so familiar worldwide that children can't wait to recite such a well-known and timeless tale. The familiarity of this children's story, combined with the alarming discovery that the Wolf is disguised in Grandmother's nightgown, creates a sense of sheer panic and delight at the same time. Whereas the Wolf in "Little Red Riding Hood" gets his due by the heroic Woodsman, the wolf in the next story is just a bit luckier.

Note

1. Charles Perrault, *Tales from Past Times, with Morals: Tales of Mother Goose* (New York: D. C. Heath, 1901).

THE BOY WHO CRIED WOLF

"The Boy Who Cried Wolf" is also known as "The Shepherd Boy and the Wolf." "The Boy Who Cried Wolf" is an Aesop's fable. A moral is delivered at the end of the story, as is true with all of Aesop's fables. Due to this fable, the phrase "to cry wolf" has become a common English idiom. The phrase "boy who cried wolf" has also become a common figure of speech. This fable is one of two Aesop's fables selected for dramatization in this book, the second being "The Lion and the Mouse." Aesop was a slave and storyteller from Greece in 620–560 BC. The longevity of this tale is indicative of its significance in literature.

"The Boy Who Cried Wolf" is not so popular with children because of the work ethic that is at the root of the story. Nevertheless, children love to act out this story because the boy gets to tell a lie repeatedly as he plays a joke on everyone. The somber ending doesn't prevent children from delighting in being in the role of the jokester, at least while the fun lasts.

And the sheep chewed some grass, rolled her eyes, and chewed some more grass.

The Story

A long time ago, but not too far away, there lived a young boy and his mother. One day Mother called to her son, "Wake up! Wake up! Wake up, son! It's time for breakfast!"

So the young boy woke up, yawned and stretched, and came down the stairs for breakfast. Mother had fixed him some oatmeal that morning. And while he ate his oatmeal, Mother said to him, "Now remember, son, you've got a very important job to do today. Your job is very important and you must take it seriously. I don't want any silly stuff. Remember that."

"Yes, Mom," said the boy. So after he finished his oatmeal, he put on his jacket, gave his mom a hug goodbye, and went out of the house, out the door, and on his way to work.

This young boy went up the hills and down the valleys. Up, up, up the hills, and down, down, down the valleys, until he came to a big grassy field. When he got to the field, he sat down on a big rock, and he began to watch the sheep. This was his job, you see. The boy's job was to watch sheep. So, he sat there and he watched, and he watched, and he watched the sheep. And the sheep chewed some grass, rolled their eyes, chewed some more grass, and the boy watched. And then he said, "Boring . . . this is so boring."

But his job was to watch sheep, so that is what he did, no matter how boring his job was. But as he watched the sheep, he had an idea. He looked down the hill, saw some men that were working in the field, and decided to play a little joke. He called down to the workmen. "Help! Help! There's a wolf! Help! Help! Hurry! A wolf!"

So the workmen down below, who heard the boy's cries, said "Quickly! The boy needs help! Let's go!" So they ran up the hill, and ran to the little boy, and said, "Where? Where? Where's the wolf? We'll get him! Stand back! Don't worry! We'll get the wolf!"

But as they looked around for the wolf, the more they searched, the more the little boy started to laugh. "Ha ha ha!" said the boy, "Hee hee hee! Ho ho ho!" laughed the boy. He laughed so hard, the louder he laughed, the angrier the workmen got.

"Young man, don't tell us you were playing a joke. This is not funny. Do not do this again. It's not funny!"

The boy said, "Okay, I won't do it." He laughed, and he tried to keep a straight face.

Well, the workmen were really upset. They marched down the hill, saying, "Never do this again." And they went back to work in the hot summer sun.

Well, about a week later, the boy was there, sitting on the rock, watching the sheep because that was his job. And, as he watched the sheep, the sheep chewed some grass, rolled their eyes, and did what sheep do most, which is not much. And the boy sat there watching the sheep and said, "Boring . . . this is so boring."

Then he had an idea. And he stood up, and he looked down the hill at the workmen, and he cried out, "Help! Help! There's a wolf! Help! Hurry! A wolf! Help me!"

The men heard the boy calling and said, "Quick! Let's go!" and they ran up the hill as fast as they could and said, "Stand back, young son! We'll get the wolf! You're safe now!"

And the men looked high, and the men looked low, and the men looked left, and the men looked right, and they couldn't find a wolf. And the boy started to laugh, but then he realized that what he did really wasn't funny, and he started to feel bad that he had tried to play a joke again.

So the workmen realized that there was no wolf and that the boy had tricked them. And they said to the boy, "You should never, never play this joke again. Never. This is not funny."

So the boy said, "I'm sorry," and he really was. "I will not play that joke again. I won't."

The workmen said, "Let's go." And they all marched down the hill.

Well, about a week later, the boy was sitting on the rock, looking at the sheep. And the sheep were chewing the grass, rolling their eyes, just being sheep. And the boy thought, "Boring. This is so boring." But he really was not going to play that joke again.

So he sat and watched the sheep because that was his job. But just then, a real wolf came from behind the trees and snuck over toward the sheep, licking his chops. The boy was really scared. And he jumped up and called down below, "Wolf! Wolf! Help! There's a wolf! I'm not kidding! There's really a wolf! Help! Help!"

And the workmen below heard the young boy's cries, but they just shook their heads and said, "That boy has not learned his lesson. He's playing a trick again. We're not going up there."

And they continued to work.

And the boy cried, "No! No! Help, it's a wolf! It really is a wolf this time! Help!" But no one came to help him.

And the wolf gobbled up the sheep, one by one. "Gulp, gulp, gulp," went the wolf.

And the poor boy learned his lesson the hard way. And that's the story of "The Boy Who Cried Wolf."

Suddenly, a real wolf came from behind the trees. . . .

Questions

- Did the boy like his job?

- How does a sheep move?

- Can you show me a sheep eating grass?

- If you were bored, how would you sit?

- When you have an idea, how does your face change expression?

- Let me see men working in the field with imaginary shovels and rakes. How would you act if it was very hot outside?

- Let me hear the boy yell so that the men can hear him all the way down the hill.

- Can you run in place as the men hear cries for help?

- Let me see you workmen searching for a wolf.

- Can you pretend to laugh like the boy?

- How angry do the workmen get?

- How can you show that they are angry?

- What makes you feel bored?

- When the boy cries "wolf" for the second time, how does he pretend to feel?

- At what point does the boy learn his lesson and regret his actions?

- Is it nice to play a trick?

- How does the wolf act when he is hungry?

- How hungry is the wolf?

- How does a sneaky and hungry wolf move?

- What does the boy do when he sees a real wolf?

- How does the boy feel when he sees the real wolf?

- Can you pretend to be a workman and ignore the boy's cries for help?

- How can we pretend that the wolf is gobbling up the sheep one by one?

- Do any of the sheep escape?

- What does the boy do now?

- Do you like the ending of this story?

- How might you change the ending?

- What would Mother say to the boy if she found out what happened?

- Could the boy explain himself?

- What does the wolf do once he is done gobbling up sheep?

Exploration

"The Boy Who Cried Wolf" is a cautionary tale. This story lends itself to dramatization very well. Children love to act out this story for several reasons, which will be explored as the story unfolds within this analysis. The story begins a long time ago, which offers safety and distance to the child from any potential harm pertaining to this tale. Notice that the story takes place "not too far away." This balances the distance, since there are no fictitious characters such as monsters, dragons, or giants that could frighten the child, only everyday and realistic characters.

"The Boy Who Cried Wolf" can easily be "The Girl Who Cried Wolf." The main protagonist doesn't have to be a boy. In fact, boys or girls should be able to play any role, regardless of gender, without jeering. It is actually healthy for boys to try on a girl's role and vice versa if they choose to do so. A child should never be forced to play a part that he or she does not want to play. It should always be left up to the child to decide. This includes prompting from a well-intentioned parent or teacher: "Would you like to be the boy?" It is important to simply let the child decide with no judgment or coercing.

As this story begins, notice that it is a child living with his mother. There is no mention of a father. Many of these classic old tales present homes run by a single parent, usually the mother—for example, "Jack and the Beanstalk," "The Three Little Pigs," and "Little Red Riding Hood," to name a few. This is appropriate in view of the number of single-parent families today.

Several children may be playing the part of the boy, which is encouraged when working with a group. Notice when the story starts that the boy is asleep. This technique is helpful in dramatizing a story with a group of children or even with just one child. Because children love to pretend to be asleep, it helps you, the storyteller, control any rambunctious or overly excitable young actors as the dramatization begins.

Mother feeds her son during the first scene of the story. The child pretends to eat breakfast using pantomime. This is very nurturing when Mother prepares a meal to feed her child. Children enjoy the act of eating imaginary food. And so our story begins with the morning routine of waking from slumber and enjoying breakfast.

Mother warns her son not to fool around on the job, foreshadowing what is to occur later in the story. Also, notice there are no specific names for any of the characters. It is mother, boy, workmen, and so on. This is done for a reason. The story is universal and timeless. The characters are representative of every woman, boy, or man by remaining generic. The characters are more relatable by being nameless.

Pantomime can be used as the boy puts on his coat and opens the door to leave. It is always more imaginative to pretend this than to utilize costumes, props, or scenery. When the boy walks up the hills and down the valleys, he can do a pantomime walk as well. This is essentially walking in place. He can lean back slightly when going up a hill and lean forward slightly when walking down the valley.

The next characters to be introduced in the story are the sheep. Before the story begins, the children can practice their sheep movements and sounds. Sheep chew grass with a lower jaw that shuffles slowly side to side. These sheep have long eyelashes that they can slowly bat as they chew. Children like to crawl around on all fours, which is appropriate for being a sheep. The baaing is a fun sound to imitate. The children playing sheep should be cued as to when to baa and when to stop the animal sounds. Running your finger across your neck or waving your hand in a horizontal fashion works well to control any animal sounds. This is necessary to allow any other dialogue to be heard. It also gives the children some parameters to work within. Encouraging creativity works best within structure.

So the boy watches the sheep. As he does so, he becomes quite bored. Boredom is an emotion that children can readily relate to. Boredom is universal, particularly in this instance of a repetitive and dull job. The boy sits on a rock to watch the sheep. He can actually sit on a chair, a beanbag chair, or the floor.

The conflict arises with the help of the boy's active imagination. He decides to play a joke on the workmen by crying "wolf." The boy pretends to call in earnest; all the while, he is actually deceitful. Furthermore, once help arrives and the boy starts to laugh, the satisfaction sets in for the children. A young boy has tricked the adults. This is quite taboo, yet children love the thought of fooling adults, if only through a story. The boy's laughter can really unleash his pure delight in this compulsive trickery.

The workmen hear the boy's calls and come running to his aid. They search high and low, to the left and right, everywhere, but no wolf. The angrier the workmen become, the harder the boy laughs, creating a great conflict of emotions. The workmen are also universal characters. Before the story begins, the children who are to play the workmen can practice shoveling and raking in the hot sun using pantomime. They are very hard workers. Once the workmen realize the boy is playing a trick, they scold him and warn him never to do it again. They try to teach him right from wrong. They march away in anger and frustration.

One week later, as the story goes, we find the boy sitting, watching the sheep again. Once again, he is bored. Children can once again relate to his boredom, as children often experience this emotion and complain about it. The repetition in the story is also comforting to children, who tend to prefer repetition within a story line in that it offers some predictability. The boy cries for help. The workmen come running to help again. The boy starts to laugh, but this time, as the workmen begin to anger, realizing it is a trick, the boy stops laughing. At this point, the boy begins to feel guilty and realizes he has made a mistake. The workmen search everywhere for the wolf and soon discover they have been tricked. They are really mad this time and give the boy a lecture on the perils of lying.

They stomp their feet, clench their fists, and yell at the boy, giving him a look he won't soon forget. They leave, vowing not to return.

By now the boy feels bad about his actions, having learned his lesson. After all, this is a famous cautionary tale. One week later, the boy is watching his sheep, and although he is bored, he knows not to play any tricks. He just does his job, boring though it may be. A wolf appears. In this case, it could be a pack of wolves, depending on how many children choose to be a wolf.

Before the story begins, the children can practice walking (sneaking) like a wolf, using howls and licking their chops. When it comes time for the wolves to chase the sheep, the children can act it out as a game of tag. If the wolf tags a sheep, then the sheep has been gobbled. The sheep then curls into a ball and rolls away. This, too, may be practiced before the story starts.

As the wolves chase the sheep, the boy calls wildly for help. The workmen hear his cries but do not come to his rescue, fearing it is another joke. They ignore his cries. One by one, the sheep get gobbled up by the wolves. The wolves lick their chops. If a sheep doesn't want to get eaten, the child can hide behind the boy in a "safety zone." A child shouldn't be forced to be gobbled up if he or she chooses not to be.

Since the story has such a sad and abrupt ending, sometimes the children request to change it. This is fine too. They might problem solve and come up with a new solution. Sometimes the children don't want the sheep to be attacked by the wolf, so they find a way to change the dire ending. Also, they might want to add a last scene with the boy and his mother after all that happens. You can try different endings.

If time permits, the story can be reenacted as children pick different parts to play. The characters in this story tend to be one-dimensional, and it is fun for children to walk in someone else's shoes. Other children do not want to switch roles, and that should always be respected.

It is said that the root of all good stories is the theme of being alone. In "The Boy Who Cried Wolf," the central protagonist, the boy, is left alone each day that he does his job of watching the sheep. It is during his time alone that the boy uses, at first, poor judgment and then goes on to redeem himself, albeit too late.

A child may love the thought of misbehaving and playing a trick on adults. This story gives the child permission to defy the rules within the safety of pretending. Also, the scene that encourages the boy to laugh wildly as the workmen rant madly is fun for children to play out. Children also love to be animals, and this story offers the sweet, docile role of the sheep, as well as the carnivorous, flesh-eating wolves: two opposing yet complementary parts. The game of tag, which is utilized within the story, adds a touch of the childhood favorite game, again within the safe confines of the story and its structure. As mentioned, children love repetition in stories, and in this story, the repetitions build until the climactic scene.

This story offers roles with dialogue, roles with animal sounds, and individual or group acting. So the variety offers something for everyone. A shy child may be content to be a docile sheep, whereas an extroverted child may opt for a character with more dialogue. The choice is theirs to make.

Tips

- "The Boy Who Cried Wolf" can easily be played by a girl to become "The Girl Who Cried Wolf."

- As the story begins, the boy or girl can be upstairs sleeping.

- There is no need to add full costumes; pantomime is more imaginative for the young actors and audience.

- The sheep can chew the grass with exaggerated jaw movements and slowly bat their eyelashes.

- Signal the sheep as to when to begin baaing and when to stop by using a simple hand gesture.

- Have everyone in the group pretend to be bored without using any words.

- Ask everyone, "How do you look when you think you have a great idea?"

- Let the child/children practice laughing and then stop them with a workman's glare. Utilize role reversal.

- The repetition in this story is comforting for young children, as they know what to expect next.

- Allow the workmen to get really angry. They can stomp their feet and clench their fists using angry voices.

- Let the wolf sneak in slowly and hungrily.

- Use a game of tag when the wolf chases and catches the sheep. When a sheep is tagged, he or she has been gobbled up.

- If a sheep doesn't want to be caught by the wolf, let the sheep be safe.

- How loudly can the boy call for help?

- This story ends rather abruptly and sadly. Do the children want to create a new ending?

- "The Boy Who Cried Wolf" can be replayed to allow the children to try on different roles.

Table 5.1. Summary of Story Elements

"The Boy Who Cried Wolf"	
Characters	The Boy (or Girl), Mother, sheep, townspeople, wolf
Inanimate Roles	Rock (optional)
Location	At home, in fields
Timeline	Long ago and not too far away
Difficulty	Moderate
Length	Short to medium
Props	n/a
Costumes	Sheep ears and tails, bells on necklaces, wolf ears and tail, apron, hats
Set	Rock for field, chair for house
Theme	Boredom, playing a trick
Plot	Mom warns boy to be good, repetition of three, climax—wolf attack
Emotions	Boredom, anger, fear
Conflict Resolution	Ends badly, boy learns valuable lesson
Pace	Slow, upbeat, slow, upbeat, slow, chaos
Moral	Don't lie

It is so much fun for children to be given permission to lie that "The Boy Who Cried Wolf" is always a heavily requested story to enact. The Boy is able to play a trick on the adults and laughs so heartily at his joke. A child pretending to laugh is going to have fun by doing so within this cautionary tale. The next story of "Jack and the Beanstalk" is no laughing matter. However, in this case, because of young Jack's perseverance, he will strike gold.

CHAPTER SIX
JACK AND THE BEANSTALK

"Jack and the Beanstalk"[1] is linked to the English fairy tale titled "Jack the Giant Killer," first published in 1711. The story as we know it today first appeared in 1734 in a book called *Round About Our Coal Fire.*[2] It was then titled "Jack Spriggins and the Enchanted Bean." Since then, hundreds of variations have been written, which have further popularized this enchanting tale.

"Bessie is our pet. We can't sell her," cried Jack.

The Story

A long time ago and very far away, there lived a little boy named Jack, who lived with his mother. They were very, very poor. One day, Mother said to Jack, "Jack, Jack, come here, Jack. Listen. I need you to take Bessie, our cow, down to the market and sell her for some money."

Jack said, "No, Mom, no. Bessie is our pet. We can't sell Bessie."

Mother said, "I'm sorry, Jack, but it's just something we have to do. We need some money to buy some food. So I really need you to do this, Jack. Just do what I say. Sell Bessie for some money, and get the best price you can get."

So Jack said, "Oh, all right, Mother." And he sadly took his pet cow, Bessie, down to the marketplace to sell Bessie for some money because they needed some food.

And then, he heard a strange little man say, "Psst, psst, young boy! Young boy! Whatcha got there?"

"I gotta sell my cow for some money," said Jack, "but I don't want to."

"I know, I know. Listen! You can sell your cow to me!"

"I can?" said Jack.

"Yes!" said the little strange man. "You can sell your cow to me and I will give you magic beans!"

"Magic beans?" said Jack.

"Magic beans!" said the strange little man. "Look! They're magical!"

"Oh, wow!" said Jack. "Magic beans! Yes, yes, I will sell you my cow for magic beans! Won't Mother be proud? Thank you so much! Sorry, Bessie."

And the little boy, Jack, put the magic beans in his pocket and was so delighted that he ran all the way home to tell his mother. "Mother, Mother! I sold the cow!"

"Oh, wonderful, Jack! I knew you would do it. I know it's sad but we had to get the money. Let me see, how much did you get? How much money did you get? Did you get some coins?"

"Well," said Jack, "No . . . not exactly."

"What do you mean, dear? Come on, show me, show me. How much money did you get for the cow? Let me see."

"Well, look, Mom, I got something better than coins. I got magic beans!" And Jack reached into his pocket and showed Mother the magic beans.

"Beans? Beans? Magic beans?! How could you?" said Mother. "What were you thinking, getting magic beans? This is ridiculous!" And she grabbed the magic beans and she threw them out the window and sent Jack to bed without any supper.

Poor Jack. He went to his room and felt terrible. He really messed up, and boy, was his mother mad! He'd never seen her so mad. So Jack went to bed without any supper. But while he slept, a funny thing happened. Outside his window, the little magical beans grew into a beanstalk. And the beanstalk grew up, up, up through the clouds into the sky. A beautiful beanstalk stood there the very next morning.

There, outside of his window, when Jack woke up, he saw the beanstalk. This beanstalk went all the way, all the way up through the clouds, into the sky, as far as the eye could see. Well, Jack jumped out of bed, leaped through the window, ran over to the beanstalk, and climbed all the way up to the very tippy top.

Once he got above the clouds, he looked and he saw a castle—a huge, giant castle. And little Jack went over to the castle, and he tapped on the door, and a big giant came to the door. It was the wife of the biggest Giant. And Jack said, "Who lives here? May I come in?"

"Oh, no, no, no," said the wife of the Giant, "Go away, little boy, you must go away. If the Giant sees you, he'll eat you for lunch, he will. Go on, be on your way." And with that, she slammed the door shut.

Well, little Jack snuck into the castle when the Giant's Wife was not looking, and he tiptoed in and hid behind the table in the kitchen. Just then, the Giant appeared, "Fee, fi, fo, fum, I smell the blood of an Englishman," said the Giant.

"Oh, don't be silly," said his wife. "There's no one here but you and me. Now then, go on about your way."

So the Giant sat down and said, "Wife, bring me my hen."

"Bock, bock, bock," said the hen.

So the wife got the hen and brought it to the Giant, her husband. And he said, "Hen, lay."

And with that, the hen laid a golden egg. And just then, the Giant fell into a deep, deep sleep.

Well, Jack couldn't believe his eyes! He had never seen a hen that could lay a golden egg. So while the Giant was sleeping, Jack tiptoed over, grabbed the hen, and ran out of the kitchen, out of the castle, across the clouds, over to the beanstalk, and all the way down the beanstalk, back to his home.

"Mother! Mother! Look!" said Jack, "Look at this!"

"Oh, Jack! Where have you been? What are you doing with that hen?"

"No, Mom, watch! It's a magic hen!"

"Why, Jack, no more of this magic talk!"

"No, no, watch, Mom!" said Jack. "Hen! Lay!"

And out popped a golden egg. "A hen that lays a golden egg? I've never seen anything like that! Where did you get that hen?" said Jack's mother.

"Mom, I went to the Giant's castle!"

"Don't talk rubbish!"

"No, I went to the Giant's castle, and he had the hen that laid the golden egg, and I took it!"

"Oh, Jack! Oh, Jack! We'll be rich from now on! With these golden eggs, we can trade them for all the food we want, and clothes, and a house! Oh, Jack, this is wonderful! But do not go back to that castle ever, ever again."

"Okay, Mom!"

But the very next day, Jack got up, jumped out of his bed, leaped through the window, and ran over to the beanstalk, climbed all the way up, went back over to the castle, snuck in through the door, tiptoed into the kitchen, and hid behind the table. Along came the Giant. "Fee, fi, fo, fum, I smell the blood of an Englishman," said the Giant.

The Giant's Wife said, "Oh, dear, there's no one here but you and me. There's no one here."

"Huh," said the Giant. "Wife, bring me my gold." So the wife brought the Giant his gold, and he began to count. "One, two, three . . . five, six . . . eight," and the Giant, while counting his gold coins, fell into a deep sleep. While he was sleeping, Jack tiptoed over, grabbed all of the gold coins, and ran out of the kitchen, out of the castle, across the clouds, over to the beanstalk, all the way down the beanstalk, and back to his home.

"Mother, Mother! Look, look, look!"

Mother came running. "Jack! Where were you? What did you do?"

"Mom, look! Gold, gold! We'll be rich, rich, rich!"

And Mother said, "Jack! Did you go back to that castle? I told you not to go and see that Giant again. You know, that

Giant and that castle where you were is the same Giant who came and took your father years ago, and these are all of our belongings that the Giant took that you are now bringing back! Nevertheless, don't go back there again! He'll have you for lunch if he catches you!"

"All right, Mother."

Mother was so happy to have the coins but begged her son not to go back.

Well, the next day Jack got up, jumped out of his bed, leaped through the window, and ran over to the beanstalk, climbed all the way up, went across the clouds over to the castle, snuck in through the door, tiptoed into the kitchen, and hid behind the table. Just then, he heard, "Fee, fi, fo, fum, I smell the blood of an Englishman."

"Don't be silly," said the Giant's Wife. "There's no one here but you and me."

"Wife," he said, "bring me my harp."

"Yes, dear." And the wife went and got the Giant's magical harp and set it down for the Giant.

The Giant said, "Sing, harp, sing!"

"Aaaah, aaaaah, ahhh!" said the harp. The harp sang the most beautiful and glorious song, and just then, the Giant fell into a deep sleep. The Giant snored.

And Jack tiptoed over, grabbed the harp, and started to run out of the kitchen, out of the castle. But the harp started to call, "Master! Master! Help! Master! Master! Help!" And the Giant woke up and saw Jack running away with his harp!

"Fee, fi, fo, fum, I did smell the blood of an Englishman, and I'm after you!" And the Giant came running after Jack.

Jack flew across the clouds, jumped on the beanstalk, still holding the harp, and went all the way down the beanstalk, calling to his mother, "Mother! Mother! Get the ax! Mother! Mother! Help!"

Mother ran and got the ax, and the Giant started to come down the beanstalk. Jack grabbed the ax. Chop, chop, chop went the ax into the beanstalk. Chop, chop, chop.

And then the beanstalk started to tip, and boom! The beanstalk fell, and the Giant came crashing to the ground, and all the way through the ground, as far as the eye could see!

And do you know, that Giant never bothered Jack or Jack's mother, ever again? And Jack and his mother lived to be very happy and wealthy and safe. And that's the story of "Jack and the Beanstalk."

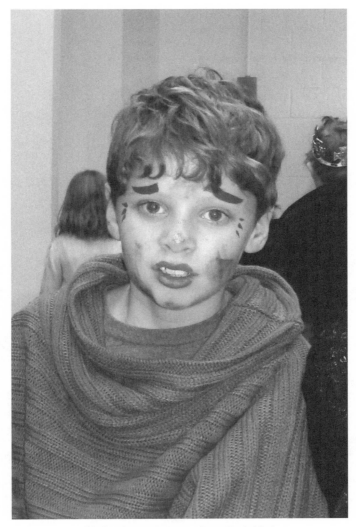

"Mother, I got some magic beans," cried Jack.

Questions

- How can you tell that Jack and his mother were poor?

- Can you move like a cow?

- Can you sound like a cow?

- How does a cow move?

- Can you chew your cud?

- How old do you think Jack is?

- How does Jack feel about selling Bessie?

- Is Bessie his pet?

- Where should we put the marketplace?

- How strange is this little man?

- What does his voice sound like?

- From where does the little man come?

- What do the magic beans look like? Describe them.

- What is Jack thinking when he sees the magic beans?

- How does Bessie feel about being sold?

- Can you pretend to run in place as Jack runs home?

- On a scale of one to ten, how mad does Mother get when she sees that Jack traded Bessie for beans instead of money?

- Can you pretend to sleep like Jack?

- Let's see how you would grow from tiny beans into a beanstalk. How can you grow taller and taller?

- What was it like for Jack to see the beanstalk?

- How can he pretend to climb the beanstalk?

- When Jack pretends to knock on the castle door, who can make the knocking sound?

- What does the castle look like?

- How do we make the Giant giant in size?

- Can you pretend to be a Giant with your body and your voice?

- Who is bigger, the Giant or his wife?

- How does Jack look as he sneaks through the castle on his tiptoes?

- Can you sneak by as quiet as a mouse?

- Let me see the Giant walk in.

- What does "fee, fi, fo, fum" mean?

- How does a hen move?

- How does a hen sound?

- What is special about this hen?

- Can you lay a golden egg?

- Let's watch the Giant sleep. What giant snoring does he do?

- Where is Jack hiding so that the Giant can't see him?

- How can Jack pretend to carry the hen as he runs out of the castle?

- Was Mother worried about Jack when he was gone?

- What did Mother think when the hen popped out a golden egg?

- How happy did Mother become knowing they would never be poor again?

- How does Jack sneak into the castle again?

- If you were the gold, how much would you be worth?

- Why doesn't Mother want Jack to go back to the castle?

- Can I hear the harp sing? How does the magical harp sound?

- Let me hear the harp call for help.

- How fast does Jack move once the Giant awakens and spots him?

- How fast can a Giant run?

- Should we do the chopping of the beanstalk in slow motion so we can watch the Giant fall slowly to the ground?

- How does the story end?

- Does the Giant ever bother Jack or his mother again?

Exploration

"Jack and the Beanstalk" is a timeless and universal fairy tale. The story begins with the introduction of a young boy named Jack. It is a poor home, as is true of many fairy tales, and once again, a single-parent family with no father. In the original version of "Jack and the Beanstalk," the father had actually been killed by the Giant before the story begins.

The fairy tale begins a long time ago and very far away, which immediately sets the pace with much needed distance for the children. This classical time frame provides a sense of distance and consequential safety.

The attraction to this story is in part based on the small and weak being wise versus the big and strong being unwise. This results in the ultimate victory for Jack and defeat for the Giant. In the real world, it is the big and strong who are wise and victorious, yet in folklore and fairy tales, it is the opposite, as the small can win.

As the story begins, Jack's mother sends Jack to sell the family cow, as they are so poor. Jack is reluctant to do so but begrudgingly takes his beloved pet cow into town to try to sell her. A child acting the role of the cow can use a cud-chewing motion for her jaw and the batting of eyelashes for some specific cow movements. Mooing can be added at optimal times in order to allow the cow to express herself. On his way to town, Jack, who could easily be played by a girl as either Jack or Jackie, is greeted by a strange little man. This man can be portrayed as a salesman type or as a magical man. He easily gets Jack to trade the cow for beans. Jack is genuinely excited about the promise of magic beans. A child can play the part of the magical beans/beanstalk as long as it is made available as an option in the role choosing process.

Jack's mother, however, is not enthusiastic about the beans at all. She throws the beans out of the window, sending Jack to bed without supper. She can actually get quite mad. Let the children decide how mad Mother should get on a scale from one to ten. Try different levels of anger through the role playing. You can always freeze and rewind the story to try a new approach.

While Jack sleeps, the beanstalk grows. Children like being a growing beanstalk. They can find ways to stretch and grow up into the sky using movement. The beanstalk can be seen as the connection between heaven and earth.

Jack awakens the next day and, being a curious and spirited young lad, he climbs the beanstalk. If a child is the beanstalk, Jack should pantomime the climbing without actually touching the beanstalk/child. Once he climbs up, he sees a castle. When Jack goes to the castle, he first meets the Giant's Wife, who at least shows some empathy toward Jack. She warns him about the Giant and what he will do if he finds Jack. Jack, however, is mischievous and daring as he sneaks into the Giant's castle despite the warning. As the Giant is introduced, he bellows his standard chant: "Fee, fi, fo, fum, I smell the blood of an Englishman." Whoever plays the part of the Giant must do so with big movements and slow, stomping feet. The Giant is characterized by his tremendous size and, in this case, small brain. A big voice can be used, and a wide stance. The leader may ask, "How can you make yourself as big as a giant?" You can actually stuff a pillow, if a play is being presented, for effect. Let the child pretend to be giant through physicality and sound. Also, you could have more than one child be the Giant, and they could move and talk in Giant unison. The child doesn't need to shout, but use a deep, booming voice for the Giant.

When the leader presents the role of the Giant, it is best to stylize the character to add distance. This is particularly true when presenting the story to young children of ages three to five. To avoid creating a truly scary Giant, you should make him be more of a big oaf, or "dumb" Giant. The actor shouldn't play the Giant realistically, but rather more like a cartoon or one-dimensional character. Any humor that can be added should be, such as when the Giant searches for Jack and can't see him right under his nose. A slow and unaware Giant gives Jack more control and an extra advantage. The Giant in folklore and fairy tales is a type of beast. He is unattractive and clearly lacking in morals. The Giant's purpose is to frighten and terrify and, in this particular tale, to devour Jack if the opportunity arises. The role of the Giant can be seen as the dark side of human nature, which is intriguing and actually healthy for children to play act. Dramatization of the role of the Giant gives children the permission to be ugly, frightening cannibals for a few minutes in an appropriate venue. When children play a scary role, they can face their own day-to-day fears in doing so. Pretending to be a beast or, in this case, a gruesome giant won't make a child become a terrible person, but, on the contrary, will allow a child to face his own fears by becoming the scary one. It is up to the individual child to select which character from any given story that he or she wants to become, rather than impose role selection.

Notice that Jack will visit the Giant's castle three times. Children enjoy the repetition, and once again the pattern of three appears in the fairy tale. The first scenario introduces the hen that lays the golden eggs. As Jack watches from his hiding place, the Giant demands that his Giant Wife bring him his magic hen. After the hen lays a golden egg, per the Giant's demand, the Giant falls into a deep, snoring sleep. Children enjoy pretending to be asleep. Jack takes the Hen and rushes out to the beanstalk and home to safety. The child pretending to be the hen can cluck and imitate a hen's neck-thrusting action. When laying a golden egg, pantomime can be used, or an actual "gold" egg may be judiciously placed, as if having been laid.

Mother scolds Jack for having gone to the Giant's castle, as she is worried about his well-being and doesn't want him in harm's way. She warns him not to go back to the castle. As the story goes, Jack doesn't heed his mother's warning and returns twice more. The next time, he takes the Giant's gold coins. Gold represents the highest of values. Gold coins represent material value. The golden eggs represent life force, and the golden harp, which is the third golden treasure, is an ethereal and celestial object to be fully revealed only when the owner plays it. The golden harp is an enticing character to become, as it is part maiden and part instrument. The child playing the role of the golden harp could sing angelically if she feels comfortable doing so. Jack succeeds in taking all three gold possessions from the Giant, but in his third attempt, the golden harp shouts out a warning to her master, the Giant, and a call for help.

The Giant awakens, and the chase is on. The Giant chases the young lad out of the castle, over to the beanstalk, and down through the clouds to Jack's very own backyard. All the while, the Giant is fee-fi-fo-fumming. The Giant is angry. Jack is a fun character to be played by a child because he is a child himself and because he is mischievous, clever, and quick on his feet. Sneaking through the castle one minute and then ultimately running for his life the next can be an exciting part to explore for a curious child. As the chase ensues, the Giant needs to move slowly and methodically so that Jack can escape and get to the bottom of the beanstalk first.

Luckily, Jack calls to his mother to grab the ax quickly, and down goes the beanstalk with the Giant crashing to his demise. It is important to mention that the Giant is now gone forever and that Jack and his mother will live happily ever after so that the children play acting the story have a sense of closure and security.

Tips

- Jack is an adventurous lad who is also a bit willful in nature.

- Jack can be played by either a boy or a girl and could even be called Jackie if preferred by the actor.

- The beans salesman is a bit sneaky and persuasive.

- The role of the beanstalk can be played by a child.

- Mother gets very angry when she sees the beans and sends Jack to bed. You and your child can rate her anger level from one to ten.

- Jack can pantomime or pretend to climb up the beanstalk, whether it is imaginary or played by a child.

- A child playing the part of the Giant loves to chant "Fee, fi, fo, fum" in a giant voice.

- Practice using slow, large movements for the Giant.

- You can stuff a pillow in the Giant's shirt for added effect if using the story as a presentation.

- When working with a group of children, you can have two or more children become the Giant collectively.

- The Giant is less threatening to young people if he is portrayed as oafish or clumsy. The "dumber" the Giant is, the smarter Jack appears to be.

- Children like to pretend to be asleep, as in the scene with the snoozing Giant.

- The hen that lays the golden eggs is a fun role to play because it is a magical bird. Use pantomimed eggs or make "gold" ones to use.

- Mother scolds Jack for going up to the castle and forbids him to go again. However, Jack doesn't listen and returns twice.

- The gold coins can be pantomimed, or you can use toy coins.

- The singing harp is part maiden and part musical instrument that tips off the Giant about Jack's thievery.

- The Giant chases but cannot catch Jack as he runs off with the harp during Jack's third and final visit to the castle.

Table 6.1. Summary of Story Elements

	"Jack and the Beanstalk"
Characters	Mother, Jack, cow, bean salesman, Giant's Wife, Giant, hen, harp
Inanimate Roles	Beans/beanstalk, golden coins
Location	Jack's home, marketplace, castle
Timeline	Long ago and far away
Difficulty	Moderate to difficult
Length	Moderate to long
Props	Ax, gold-colored materials
Costumes	Cow ears and tail, hats or caps, vest, pillows for stuffing, oversized clothes, hen wings, leaves for beanstalk
Set	Beanstalk, castle
Theme	Small versus giant—success
Plot	Repetitious
Emotions	High intensity, anger, fear, life-threatening
Conflict Resolution	Repeated conflict—positive resolution
Pace	High
Moral	Small can overcome giant using wit and determination

- As Mother chops down the beanstalk, the Giant falls in slow motion to his untimely, yet deserved, demise.

"Jack and the Beanstalk" has many magical elements to it, including the beanstalk, the castle, the Giant, and the Golden Harp, making it a great story to act out. It is well known and full of repetition, which children really do enjoy. The sneaking about and the buildup to the climactic fall of the Giant make "Jack and the Beanstalk" an excellent choice for play acting. The only sneaking about in the next story is by the little hero called the Mouse.

Notes

1. *Jack the Giant Killer* (Newcastle, England: J. White, 1711).
2. W. H. Davenport Adams, *Round About Our Coal Fire: Or Christmas Entertainments*, 2nd ed. (London: J. Roberts, 1734).

CHAPTER SEVEN
THE LION AND THE MOUSE

"The Lion and the Mouse" is also an Aesop fable. The story itself actually dates back to 1166 BC. It is one of the oldest stories in this collection of tales used for dramatization purposes. It is one of Aesop's most popular fables, and has clearly withstood the test of time. As a slave, Aesop cleverly used only animals in his story to comment on the plight of human beings. Like all of Aesop's fables, "The Lion and the Mouse" teaches a moral.

"The Lion and the Mouse" is another example of the very small overcoming huge obstacles to succeed and, in this case, survive. The fable is short and simple, yet highly significant in meaning. It is a wonderful choice for play acting because the dialogue is minimal and the story can be based primarily on the physical action and the narration of the leader.

"Squeak, squeak!" said the Mouse. "Squeak, squeak! I will help you!"

The Story

A long time ago, but not too far away, deep in the jungle there lived the king of the jungle, a mighty Lion. One day, the Lion was sitting in the jungle, and he thought to himself, "Rawr, I am so hungry. Rawr. But there's nothing to eat. Hmph. I guess I will just take a nap."

And with that, the king of the beasts curled up into a ball, yawned and stretched, closed his eyes, and fell into a deep, deep sleep. As the Lion was sleeping, along came a teeny, tiny Mouse. The Mouse was crossing through the jungle on his way home. He tiptoed by the Lion, careful not to wake him up. But as the Mouse crept by, the mighty Lion opened his eyes, grabbed the Mouse by the tail, and said, "Rawr! Ha, ha! Now I finally can have some lunch!"

And he held the little Mouse by the tail, opened his mighty jaws, and was ready to have the Mouse as a snack. The Mouse said, "Oh, please, oh, please, Lion, don't eat me! Please set me free!"

But the Lion was ready to eat the Mouse. "No! Please set me free! Please! If you set me free," said the Mouse, "then I will do something for you one day. I promise I will. I'll return the favor. I know I can do it."

"Ha, ha, ha!" laughed the Lion. "Rawr! Ha, ha, ha! That's so funny!" Well, he thought it was so funny that the Lion did set the Mouse free. He dropped him onto the ground.

And the little Mouse said, "Thank you, thank you! Squeak! Squeak!" And the little Mouse ran away as quickly as he could, so happy to be free from the Lion's jaws.

Well, the Lion didn't have lunch that day but continued to take his nap. So he yawned, and stretched, and closed his eyes, and chuckled to himself about the little Mouse. And as he closed his eyes and fell into a deep sleep, along came two men. And these two men were in a truck. In the truck, they drove up, and one said, "Come on, let's go find us a lion! Come on, Ed."

"All right, Joe," said the other, scratchin' and itchin'. "Let's go find us a lion."

So the two men, Joe and Ed, walked deep into the jungle, looking and searching to find themselves a lion. No sooner had they gone into the jungle than they saw the king of the beasts, the mighty Lion, sleeping by a tree. And Joe said, "Gimme a net!"

Ed said, "Here it is!"

And they took the net, and they threw the net over the Lion. "Rawr!" said the Lion. He woke up and he jumped to his feet, but he couldn't move because he was caught in the net. "Rawr!" said the Lion. "Let me go!"

Joe and Ed said, "Ha, ha, ha! We caught us a lion! Let's go get the truck. He's a mighty fine lion."

So Joe and Ed went back through the jungle to get their truck. While they were gone, the poor Lion struggled to free himself from the net, but he could not do it. He started to feel very sad. But just about that time, the little Mouse came by again.

"Squeak, squeak!" went the Mouse. "Squeak, squeak! I will help you!"

And the Lion looked down sadly and said, "There's nothing you can do. I've been caught."

But the Mouse began to chew on the net. He began to gnaw away at the net, bit by bit. And do you know that that Mouse was able to chew through the net and made a big, large hole in the net, big enough for the Lion to get out, and the Lion escaped? And the Lion said to the Mouse, "You are a true friend. I'm so grateful that you did this for me. I will always owe you. I will always be your true friend."

The Lion and the Mouse ran deep into the jungle, but they peeked back to see what happened next. And just then, Joe and Ed returned in their truck. "Vroom, vroom!" went the truck. They got out of the truck and they shut the doors, and they itched and scratched, and they came over to get themselves a lion and put it in the truck. But when they got there, the net was empty!

Joe said, "Hey, Ed! Where's the lion?"

And Ed said, "Uh, where . . . where's the lion? Wait a minute! The lion's gone!"

They picked up the net, and they shook the net, and they saw the hole. The Lion had escaped! And Joe and Ed never did catch a lion that day. And they fussed and grumbled on their way home.

But do you know that that Lion and that little Mouse became fast friends—friends for life?

And that's the story of "The Lion and the Mouse."

The little mouse was so happy to be free. . . .

127

Questions

- Who can roar like a lion?

- Who can move like the king of the jungle?

- How does a lion sound when he is snoring?

- Who can be a sleeping lion?

- What sound does a mouse make?

- How can you make yourself tiny like a mouse?

- Who can tiptoe like a mouse?

- How can we pretend the Lion is holding the Mouse by the tail?

- Who can beg the Lion to set him free? What would you say?

- Let's hear the Lion laugh. Can you laugh like a lion?

- How does the Mouse feel when the Lion sets him free?

- Can you sneak through the jungle searching for a lion, like Joe and Ed?

- Can you pretend that you don't know the Lion is there and discover him by surprise?

- How many children does it take to be a net?

- Once the Lion is caught, how does he feel? Is he mad? Sad?

- Can you struggle to be free of the net like the Lion?

- Can I see you as the Mouse pretending to chew on the net?

- How did the Lion feel to be freed?

- How did the Mouse feel to free the Lion?

- Who can be the sounds of the truck?

- Can you pantomime the steering wheel and doors?

- Can friends come in all different shapes and sizes, just like the Lion and the Mouse?

Exploration

Children love this story because it is about the small and meek versus the large and brave—the smarts of the small Mouse overcoming the brawn of the undefeatable king of the jungle. And further, it is about the friendship that develops among nature's enemies in the face of fear.

The story begins with the mighty Lion growling with hunger, yet taking a catnap. Pretending to be a lion involves moving like a wild cat in a slinky and predatory fashion. The mane and the claws of the Lion can be a central focus of the animal's energy for the child actor.

Before the story begins, the children can practice moving, sounding, and thinking like the powerful Lion. The Lion's growl when he is hungry may sound different from when he is angry and so on. Also, the Lion's attitude can be explored to include powerfulness, prowess, royalty, hunger, aggression, or beastliness. The Mouse and all of his opposite traits may be explored too, the movements being very small and done with a scurrying motion. Tiny squeaks may be vocalized by the children as a warm-up phase before the story acting. Mice also have tiny chewing movements with protruding teeth that are particularly integral to this story.

The Lion curls up in a ball as a house cat would and falls asleep. You could have a pride of Lions or a group of Mice, and this is completely acceptable for dramatization purposes. As the Lion sleeps, along tiptoes a tiny Mouse (or group of Mice). The Lion may even snore as the Mouse creeps by. As the Mouse crosses right in front of the Lion, the Lion awakes and grabs the Mouse with one paw. Again, the Lion can gently tag the Mouse to indicate catching him. Since the Lion can't actually lift the Mouse by the tail, he can simply hold the Mouse under his paw, or, if a fake tail is used, the Lion can hold the Mouse by his tail. The tiny Mouse begs for his life, promising to return the favor one day to the Lion if he sets him free.

The Lion laughs heartily at such a ridiculous plea but, being in a lighthearted state of mind, sets the Mouse free. Here we have fear and pleading in the face of raucous laughter, a conflicting set of emotions.

However, the Mouse gets his freedom, which results in relief as he scampers off as quickly as possible while remembering his promise.

The Lion can actually roll around on his back as he is laughing so hard. In fact, he has laughed so hard that he has tired himself out. The Lion then yawns and stretches and falls asleep again while still chuckling. The Lion is in a deep sleep as he takes a catnap.

He doesn't hear the truck drive up. Someone can be the truck or make the truck noises. The two men are best portrayed as cartoon characters or one-dimensional roles. They are the antagonists of the story, or the bad guys. They are not too smart or too kind—buffoons. They can be played for comic relief if they are played in a slapstick manner—scratching their heads and ribs. The two men are going to be outsmarted by the animals.

The two men are looking high and looking low as they search for a lion. Children can become the trees in the jungle if they like. They could be the trees as an ensemble or even as a chorus, commenting on the men's actions. The men see the Lion but the Lion doesn't see them, for he is sleeping soundly when they find him.

The net can be played by a child or children, which can be fun when capturing and containing the Lion. The net can also be pantomimed. If children are being the net, the Lion can only pretend to escape gently or in slow motion so as not to physically hurt the child-net. The net may pretend to cover the Lion, but only in the air and without touching the Lion, to prevent any rough play. The Lion is upset when he awakens to find himself captured by the net. Once the Lion has been captured, the strong and powerful becomes the weak. The two men can laugh with happiness.

The Lion goes from angry to sad and feels discouraged and hopeless. The men go back through the jungle to get their truck. Just then, the little Mouse returns. One can use a squeaky mouse voice combining the English language with interjected squeaks. The Lion has lost all hope, and his body shows this by collapsing. The Mouse sizes up the situation in a split second and knows just what to do. The Mouse, who was once weak, is now the powerful one because of his cunning and his sharp teeth. There is a moment of decision-making, and the Mouse begins the pantomimed chewing action. He gnaws swiftly and with purpose. If two children are playing the net, they can fall to each side, having been chewed apart. If one child is playing the net, he can collapse to one side in a pile. If the net is pantomimed, the narrator can simply describe that a large hole has been chewed by the Mouse. The Lion is thrilled to have escaped and can let out a mighty roar at that moment of freedom. The Lion thanks the Mouse in a heartfelt way for saving his life.

The Lion and Mouse are now safe and can watch what transpires next from the safety of the nearby jungle. When the two men return to find the empty net, they are dumbfounded. They do not have a clue as to what has happened. They do not know where the Lion is. The men grumble and mumble as they leave, never again to return.

The Lion and the Mouse are now fast friends. A hug or a handshake and an overall feeling of contentment can indicate this friendship. The Lion and the Mouse are an unlikely twosome because in many ways they are opposites. Their paths crossed in a time of life-threatening circumstances for each of them. Note that the Lion and the Mouse are not given names, so their generic status and universality is maintained. This story focuses on the strong versus the weak and the role reversal of the stated status. Although quite short, the story is inherently meaningful. It can be played repeatedly so that the children can try on different roles.

Tips

- Before the enactment begins, allow the children to move like a lion. Lions move in a slinky and predatory fashion with almost a shoulder roll.

- See how being the king of the jungle affects the Lion's movements and his attitude—for example, status, power, and royalty.

- Allow the children to practice moving like a mouse before the story enactment begins. A mouse's movements are quite small, and it scurries. The Mouse's movements and thoughts are actually the opposite of the Lion's.

- Being a mouse requires tiny chewing motions, as the gnawing is important to the story.

- The squeaking of the Mouse and the thunderous roaring of the Lion can also be explored before dramatizing the story.

- There can be one Lion and one Mouse, or a pride of Lions and a group of Mice, depending on the size of the group of children.

- The Lion curls up in a ball to sleep, as a cat would, and may even snore for effect.

- The Lion can tag the Mouse as he awakens to represent catching the little creature.

- If the Mouse has a fake tail, the Lion can gently hold it to represent dangling the Mouse by its tail, or the Lion can hold the Mouse under one paw.

- It is fun for the Lion to laugh heartily, and this can be practiced before the actual dramatization.

- The Mouse scampers away as quickly as he can once he is set free by the Lion. Children can run on all fours or on two legs, whichever is easier.

- Someone can be the truck or make the truck's noises.

- The two hunters are to be portrayed as being not too smart, since they are the antagonists of the story.

- Depending on the size of the group, one can have children become the trees of the jungle, complete with cued vocal warnings.

- A child can be the net, or the net can be pantomimed.

- If a child is pretending to be the net, the Lion can only try to escape gently, so as not to physically hurt the other child, or slow motion can be used.

- When the Lion loses all hope of escaping from the net, his body collapses in defeat.

- The Mouse, making good on his word, uses the previously rehearsed gnawing technique without actually using any physical contact.

- Once the net is chewed, it falls in a pile.

- The Lion lets out a happy roar when he is finally free.

- After the Lion is freed, he and his new best friend, the Mouse, find a safe place to hide while watching the rest of the story unfold.

- The two men are confused and dumbfounded to find the Lion has escaped. They indicate this through dialogue and physical action, for example, scratching their heads.

- The Lion and the Mouse can "high five" or have a "paw-shake" to cement their friendship and solidify the newly formed bond.

Table 7.1.   Summary of Story Elements

"The Lion and the Mouse"	
Characters	Lion, Mouse, two men
Inanimate Roles	Net, truck, forest
Location	Jungle
Timeline	Long ago and not too far away
Difficulty	Simple
Length	Short
Props	n/a
Costumes	Lion ears and tail, mouse ears and tail, two hats
Set	n/a
Theme	All good deeds will be returned, the small can be big in many ways
Plot	Fable format
Emotions	Fear, trapped, freedom
Conflict Resolution	Lion gets caught, Mouse saves him
Pace	Methodical
Moral	Don't underestimate the power of the small

"The Lion and the Mouse" is not flashy or complex, but the beauty of this story lies in the simplicity of the small and meek overcoming great obstacles in order to help the big and masterful. Children enjoy being in a small and seemingly insignificant role only to wind up succeeding in the end. This story is a perfect example of that. As the Mouse nibbles the net for the Lion's freedom, the next heroes, Hansel and Gretel, nibble their way to danger.

CHAPTER EIGHT
HANSEL AND GRETEL

"Hansel and Gretel" was written by Jacob and Wilhelm Grimm (the Brothers Grimm). Born and raised in Germany, they wrote their first book, the previously mentioned *Children's and Household Tales,*[1] in 1812. This collection contained eighty-six tales, including "Hansel and Gretel." "The Wolf and the Seven Kids" and "Little Red Riding Hood" are also found in this collection. Later editions of *Children's and Household Tales* contained two hundred tales. Nearly two centuries later, this story is as entertaining and enticing as ever. The protagonists are siblings Hansel and Gretel, and the infamous antagonist is the Witch who lives in the gingerbread house. Since its first introduction in 1812, "Hansel and Gretel" has been adapted into plays, movies, musicals, and operas.

The story of Hansel and Gretel begins with poverty and abandonment, hunger and survival. Children are drawn to this fairy tale because the children themselves outsmart the cunning Witch. The young protagonists face danger and life-threatening situations, only to survive the impossible.

"Look, Hansel; a house made of all candy!" cried Gretel.

The Story

A long time ago and very far away, there lived a little boy named Hansel and a little girl named Gretel. They lived in a house with their father and stepmother. They were very, very poor. They didn't have much to eat. All they had were some breadcrumbs, and they slept on a single mat on the floor.

One night, when they were upstairs going to sleep, Gretel said to Hansel, "Psst! Wake up, Hansel, wake up! Listen, listen, it's Stepmother!"

And they could hear their stepmother down below saying to Father, "Tomorrow morning, we're going to take the children out to the woods and leave them there. We don't have enough food to keep them, the decision has been made."

"But," said Father, "they're our children!"

"Nope," said the stepmother, "there's nothing else that we can do. Tomorrow it is."

Well, when Gretel heard this, she started to cry, "Oh, oh no!"

And Hansel said, "No, no, no, Gretel, listen, everything will be fine. I have an idea."

They could hardly sleep. They tossed and turned, but the next morning when they woke up, they went downstairs. The stepmother said, "Children, Hansel, Gretel, we're going out to the woods today to take a nice family walk."

"Yes, Stepmother," said Hansel. Gretel was still very upset. And off they went into the woods: Father, Stepmother, Hansel, and Gretel.

"Hansel, Gretel, make yourselves useful. Go gather some sticks, we need some sticks, and some berries for dinner. Please, go do some work right now," scolded the stepmother.

So Hansel and Gretel turned to get some sticks and some berries, and when they turned back, their father and wicked stepmother were gone. Gretel began to cry. "Oh, oh no, they're gone. What do we do now?"

And Hansel said, "Don't worry Gretel, I have a plan. See these breadcrumbs? I dropped them and made a path, so all we have to do is follow the path back out of the woods and we'll be home again, safe and sound. Come on, Gretel, let's go!"

But as Hansel turned and Gretel followed, he saw the breadcrumbs were no longer there. "Hansel, what are you talking about? I don't see any breadcrumbs."

"But, but, I had the breadcrumbs, I dropped them along the way. I left us a little trail and . . ."

"Caw! Caw!" There was a crow. He had the last breadcrumb in his mouth. You see, the black crow had flown by and eaten all the breadcrumbs, and now they were truly lost in the middle of the woods, left all alone. Gretel was really getting upset.

"No, we'll think of something, Gretel. I'll think of something. Don't worry." And just then, a little dove flew overhead. It was white and very beautiful. "Look, Gretel, the dove wants us to follow him. Let's go!"

And as they followed the dove through the woods, suddenly they turned and looked up and saw the most amazing thing! It was a house—but it was no ordinary house. The house was made of gingerbread! Hansel and Gretel ran as fast as they could to the gingerbread house. There were gumdrops, candy canes, jellybeans, chocolate, and toffee, anything that you could think of—a whole house made of candy! And Hansel and Gretel began to nibble. "Oh, Gretel, this is delicious!"

"Mmmm," said Gretel, "try some of this!" And Hansel and Gretel nibbled and chewed and nibbled and chewed and really just filled their bellies with the delicious candy house. There was licorice, there was peanut brittle, everything you can imagine. But just then, there was a sound from inside the house.

"Nibble, nibble like a mouse, who's that nibbling on my house?"

Hansel and Gretel kept eating. "Mmmm, try this. Mmmm, delicious. Mmmm, this is peanut butter!"

"Nibble, nibble like a mouse, who's that nibbling on my house?" And just then, an old, old woman came and opened the door and peeked out. "Oh, children I see," she said.

"Well, I'm Hansel."

"And I'm Gretel."

"Oh, come in, come in, you must be hungry."

"Uh, yes," said Hansel, "we are hungry. Sorry about your house."

"Don't worry, children. Come in, come in."

So Hansel and Gretel went into the house, not knowing that the woman was a witch. They sat down, and the Witch said, "Here's some food for you. Here are some sandwiches. Eat all that you want. I must plump you up."

Well, they were so hungry that they ate, and ate, and ate. But Gretel thought, "Plump us up?"

And then, before you knew it, the Witch took Hansel, pushed him into a cage, and locked the door. "Ha, ha, ha," said the Witch. "Now I've got you just where I want you. I'm going to plump you up, and when you're nice and fat, I'll have you for dinner. And you, little girl," she said to Gretel, "you'll be my slave and do everything I want. Ha, ha, ha."

Well, what were they going to do now? Hansel was locked in the cage and every morning, the Witch went over to feel his arm to see if he was plumper. But Gretel had snuck a bone to him, so he held the bone out, and since everyone knows witches have terrible eyesight, the Witch felt the bone and thought Hansel was still too thin. "Oh, you're still too thin. Let's plump you up. We've got to cook a big meal."

So the Witch went over to light the oven and said to Gretel, "Come here, little girl, crawl into this oven and light it and make sure it's nice and hot."

Gretel said, "Oh, uh, I don't think I know how. Can you show me?"

The Witch sighed, "All right then."

As the Witch leaned into the oven to show Gretel what to do, Gretel pushed her into the oven and shut the door, and the Witch was no more. And, as the Witch baked in the oven, Hansel became free, and all of the little gingerbread cookies that surrounded the house unfroze. They turned into all of the little children that had gone missing from the village over the years.

Also, Hansel and Gretel found a big box filled with treasures

and riches—the money that the Witch stole from their father

and mother many years ago. So Hansel and Gretel took all of

the treasures and riches home with them, and they lived happily

ever after.

And that's the story of "Hansel and Gretel."

"Nibble, nibble like a mouse. Who's that nibbling on my house?"

Questions

- How can you tell that Hansel and Gretel are so poor?

- Is the stepmother wicked?

- Why does the stepmother want to leave the children in the woods?

- How old do you think Hansel and Gretel are?

- What do they think when they overhear the stepmother's wicked plan?

- What is Father thinking?

- What happened to the trail of breadcrumbs that Hansel made?

- How did Hansel and Gretel spot the gingerbread house?

- What types of candy is the gingerbread house made of?

- If you are pretending to be the Gingerbread Kids outside of the gingerbread house, can you stand stiffly like a cookie and not blink? Like a statue?

- How much candy can you pretend to eat?

- Did Hansel and Gretel like eating the candy house?

- Did Hansel and Gretel know it was a witch at first?

- Can you make your voice sweet like the Witch when she is trying to trick Hansel and Gretel?

- How does the Witch move?

- What did Hansel and Gretel think when the old woman came out of the house and caught them eating?

- When did Hansel and Gretel know it was a witch?

- How can we make a cage for Hansel to be in?

- Why didn't Hansel plump up?

- Who saves the day?

- What can we use for the oven?

- How happy are Hansel and Gretel when the Witch is no more?

- How does this story end?

Exploration

This classic fairy tale is a wonderful choice for dramatization because it is rich with subtext. "Hansel and Gretel" is a many-layered story that has been passed down over the years. This story is more complicated than some of the other tales described in this book. It deals with abandonment, isolation, poverty, and temptation. It is famous for the young heroes out-smarting their wicked captor.

As the tale begins, we find Hansel and Gretel almost asleep as they overhear their stepmother tell of a plan to drop them into the woods the next day. The family is so poor that there is not enough food for everyone to survive. Having overheard the plan for their potential demise, Hansel cleverly drops breadcrumbs to leave a trail in the woods so that they can find their way out. Unfortunately, a bird eats the crumbs, and they are truly lost in the woods. Gretel begins to cry, and Hansel tries to comfort her. As the brother and sister stand alone, deep in the woods, another bird flies by and seems to beckon Hansel and Gretel to follow him. As they follow the bird, they see the infamous gingerbread house. They are so hungry by this time that they cannot resist eating the gingerbread house. Children can pretend to be the actual gingerbread house. In one version of the story, the house turns back into children after the Witch dies, as her spell becomes undone. The siblings continue to pantomime the eating of the gingerbread house. They can improvise discovering their favorite candies and devouring them one by one, "Gumdrops, licorice, candy corn, chocolate," and so on. Have the children call out a favorite candy as they see it and then eat it. This scene of eating the candy house is every child's dream—until the children hear a wicked voice from within.

"Nibble, nibble like a mouse, who is that nibbling at my house?"

The children drop what they are eating and look up to see an old woman at the door. She invites them in and proceeds to feed them, the ulterior motive being to plump them up, particularly Hansel. She is very nice to Hansel and Gretel, who don't realize she has lured them to her candy house in order to capture, cook, and ultimately eat them.

As the story unfolds from within the gingerbread house, the Witch grabs Hansel and locks him in a cage. Children can pretend to be the actual cage, linking arms to keep him locked in. Gretel unwillingly becomes the Witch's servant. The Witch has poor vision and doesn't realize that Hansel is only using a chicken bone for her to feel instead of his actual arm. This delays the Witch from attempting to cook Hansel until she believes he gets fatter. A pencil can easily be used in practice as the chicken bone. As the story goes, Gretel outsmarts the Witch by pushing her inside the oven and freeing Hansel. Again, in working with a group of children, they can become the oven that captures and demolishes the Witch forever.

Hansel and Gretel are now free, and they take all of the precious jewels from the Witch's home. They run home to share their triumph with their parents and live happily ever after.

This is in part a story of rags to riches, as they start out in sheer poverty and end up wealthy due to their quick thinking. The story begins with not enough food to feed the family, only to be countered by the discovery of a candy house, a house made of delectable treats in an all-you-can-eat fashion. In addition to their initial dire need, the siblings find themselves abandoned by their own parents, albeit a wicked stepmother. The children are left alone to their own devices in the woods. They are lost—a very difficult situation indeed. But worse is having been captured by the horrible Witch, who plans to devour Hansel. Hansel becomes a victim while Gretel ultimately outsmarts the Witch.

This fairy tale is more advanced than most. The Witch is a more highly developed character than the Wolf. A Wolf is expected to attack, whereas the Witch is human and calculating. She is a more difficult adversary than the Wolf or the bumbling Giant. But, as in most fairy tales, the children outsmart the antagonist and go on to live happily ever after.

Tips

- Hansel and Gretel can be falling asleep as the story begins, but once they overhear their stepmother's plan, they awaken and eavesdrop, unbeknown to the father and stepmother.

- Hansel can pantomime leaving a trail of breadcrumbs that a bird later eats.

- Once they have been abandoned in the woods with no breadcrumb trail remaining, Hansel must console his sister, who is visibly upset.

- Another bird, to be played by a child, shows Hansel and Gretel the way to the gingerbread house by soaring by and beckoning to them.

- The gingerbread house can be played by gingerbread children or it can be easily pantomimed.

- The more the narrator describes the candy house, the more Hansel and Gretel devour it.

- The Witch's voice from within the house is that of an old woman.

- Children can become the cage that holds Hansel or the oven that ultimately destroys the Witch.

- The dialogue among the three characters becomes heightened once Hansel and Gretel discover the Old Woman's true identity and motivation.

- The Witch is very old and cannot see too well, which is to Hansel and Gretel's advantage.

- Hansel and Gretel can stage-whisper their plans to escape to each other so that the audience can hear but the Witch cannot.

- Once Hansel is captured inside the cage, Gretel becomes the Witch's slave but has an idea as to how to outsmart the Witch.

- Once the Witch gets pushed into the oven and dies, the children that had become the gingerbread house come back to life.

- A celebration with song or dance can ensue.

- The Witch's riches are retrieved by Hansel and Gretel via pantomime, and once they return home they live happily ever after.

Table 8.1. Summary of Story Elements

"Hansel and Gretel"	
Characters	Father, Stepmother, Hansel, Gretel, Witch, birds
Inanimate Roles	Cookie children, house, cage, oven
Location	Poor house, deep in the woods
Timeline	Long ago and far away
Difficulty	Complex
Length	Long
Props	Breadcrumbs, bone, jewels
Costumes	Vests, hats, witch attire, bird wings
Set	Gingerbread house
Theme	Poverty, greed, cunning
Plot	Rags to riches, happy ending, conflict and resolution
Emotions	Dark, heavy issues
Conflict Resolution	Gretel saves Hansel from the Witch
Pace	Steady and methodical
Moral	Goodness outsmarts wickedness

A well-known story that has stood the test of time, "Hansel and Gretel" is clearly a highly dramatic story, compelling for children to dramatize. The discovery of and the consequent devouring of the gingerbread house is a memorable scene to improvise. This story is a rags-to-riches story that ends happily. The next story, "The Three Little Pigs," also has a happy ending, but not without its share of storm and strife.

Note

1. Jacob Ludwig Carl Grimm and Wilhelm Carl Grimm, *Grimms' Fairy Tales: Forty-two Household Tales* (Charleston, SC: Forgotten Books, 2008).

THE THREE LITTLE PIGS

Although first printed in the 1840s, "The Three Little Pigs" is thought to be a much older tale. The first publication was in a book titled *Popular Rhymes and Nursery Tales*[1] by James Orchard Halliwell-Phillipps. The best-known version of the story is in Joseph Jacob's book *English Fairy Tales*,[2] published in 1890. There are many versions of this classic tale, including the award-winning Disney cartoon, which was modernized in 1933.

"The Three Little Pigs" is another great choice to enact because of its familiarity and also because of its run-for-your-life moments. It is not the work ethic or moralizing that attracts children to this classic story. Rather, it is the sheer chaos that results each time that the wolf succeeds in blowing down a pig's house. The chase scenes are high-energy and action-packed fun to dramatize.

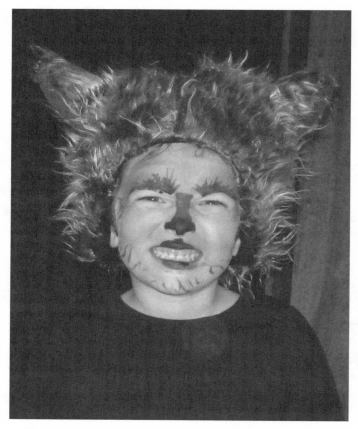

"I'm going to huff and puff and blow your house down!" cried the Wolf.

The Story

A long time ago and very far away, there lived a mama pig and her three little pigs. One morning, Mother called to her little piggies to wake up. "Wake up! Wake up, children!"

And the three little piggies yawned, stretched, woke up, and came downstairs for breakfast. Mother fed her three piggies some slops, and they ate it up. Just then, Mother said to the three piggies, "Piggies! My three sons, today is an important day. You shall go out into the big, wide world and make your own home, and make your own way."

The three piggies said, "Oh, Mom."

"Nope," she said. "None of that. It's time to go out into the big, wide world."

And with that, the three little piggies went off on their merry way. As they walked along, the youngest piggy heard someone say, "Pssst, pssst, hey you! Piggy! Come here, piggy!"

And the little pig looked, and he walked over to a man. The man said, "You wanna build a house? I can sell you some straw."

And the littlest piggy said, "Yeah, I'd like to buy some straw! I do gotta make a house. And my mom gave me this coin. Here, it's for you now, and I will buy some straw and build a house."

So the littlest piggy took the straw in a wheelbarrow from the strange old man and wheeled it over to a spot he picked, and he threw together a straw house lickety-split! Just like that! A house made of straw for the youngest pig. Then he sat down and drank some lemonade. He was done.

The second little piggy was walking along his merry way when he heard the strange old man say, "Psst, psst, piggy! Hey, you, piggy! Come here, come here!"

And the pig said, "Yes?"

The man said, "You wanna buy some sticks?"

"Yes," said the pig. "How did you know? I do need to make a house, and sticks sound just right. My mother gave me this coin. Now you can have it, and I will take some sticks."

So the second piggy took some sticks in a wheelbarrow, found a spot, and lickety-split, built himself a house of sticks, just like that! Then he sat down and drank some lemonade. He was done with his work. All done.

Well, the third piggy was a little older, and a little smarter. He heard the strange man say. "Psst, psst, come here, piggy. Hey piggy, you wanna buy some straw to build your house?"

"Straw?" said the smartest pig. "No way. I don't want straw to build a house. That's ridiculous."

"Would you like to buy some sticks to build a house?"

"Sticks to build a house?" said the third pig. "No, I don't want sticks. Don't be ridiculous."

"Hmm," said the strange man. "How would you like to buy some bricks?"

"Bricks," said the oldest, smartest pig. "Now you're talking. Yes, I would like to buy some bricks, and I have some money right here. Some coins from my mother."

So the oldest pig bought some bricks and took them in a wheelbarrow, and he worked day in and day out, day out and day in, building a house with the bricks and cement and working very, very hard to build a strong, durable, safe house. It took him a very, very long time. Finally, the house was done. And then the pig sat down, took a break, and had some lemonade.

Well, just about that time, there was a mean, old, sneaky Wolf coming through the woods. And the Wolf saw a house of straw that the youngest pig had made. And the Wolf came up to the house and said, "Let me in, let me in!"

And inside, the littlest pig said, "Not by the hair of my chinny chin chin!"

And outside, the Wolf said, "Well, then I'm going to huff, and I'm going to puff, and I'm going to blow your house in!" "Whooooooo," went the Wolf, and the straw went flying everywhere. The poor little pig was running as fast as he could, hightailing it over to his brother's house of sticks.

"Let me in! Quickly, quickly! Let me in!" said the littlest pig. "Oh, brother, the Wolf is after me! He blew down my house of straw!"

The brother said, "Oh! Well, we're in a house of sticks; we should be okay, right?"

Well, the Wolf came up to the house of sticks and said, "Let me in, let me in!"

"Not by the hair of our chinny chin chins!" said the pig brothers.

"Well, then I'm going to huff, and I'm going to puff, and I'm going to blow your house in!" said the Wolf. "Whooooooo," went the Wolf, and the sticks went flying everywhere! The two pigs really had to hightail it out of there. They ran as fast as two little pigs could run, and the Wolf was chasing them.

When they got to their oldest brother's house, the house of bricks, they ran inside to safety and said, "Brother pig, brother pig! The wolf is after us! He blew down my house of straw!"

"And he blew down my house of sticks!"

"Don't worry," said the oldest pig, "you'll be safe here. My house is made of bricks."

Then the Wolf came to the door. "Let me in, let me in!"

"Not by the hair of our chinny chin chins!" said the pig brothers.

"Well, then I'm going to huff, and I'm going to puff, and I'm going to blow your house in!" said the Wolf. "Whoooooo," went the Wolf. "Whooooooo." He huffed, and he puffed, but he could not blow the house down. So he tried again. "Whoooooooo." He could not blow down the house of bricks. It was too strong.

But the Wolf had an idea. He climbed up on the roof and climbed over to the chimney. Just then, the oldest pig said, "Quickly, let's act fast!"

And they grabbed a big, bubbling pot and put it beneath the chimney, in the fireplace. Just at that time, the Wolf came crawling down the chimney, and he landed in the big, bubbling pot.

Splash! went the Wolf. And the pigs got the lid, and put it on top of the big, black pot, and captured that mean, old, nasty Wolf. And do you know that that Wolf never, ever bothered any of the pigs again?

And the three pigs lived very happily ever after. And they visited their mom every Sunday.

And that's the story of "The Three Little Pigs."

"Not by the hair of our chinny-chin-chins!" shouted the pigs.

Questions

- How does this fairy tale begin?

- Can you pretend to be fast asleep?

- When you wake up, is it slow? Can you pretend to yawn and stretch?

- What does Mother feed her piggies for breakfast?

- Why is today such an important day?

- What do the three piggies think about going out into the big, wide world?

- What is the man like whom the pigs meet?

- What does the first, youngest pig buy to build his house?

- Is it a good idea to build a house with straw?

- If someone wants to be the straw house, let's see how you would stand or bend.

- Let me see the youngest pig drink his lemonade.

- Is this pig a bit lazy? Do we know?

- Is the second pig happy to buy sticks for his house?

- How does the stick house look?

- How fast does he build the stick house?

- Who is the smartest pig?

- Are bricks a good choice for home building?

- The oldest pig took a very long time to build his house of bricks. Will his house be the strongest?

- How sneaky is the Wolf?

- Is the Wolf hungry too?

- What does the littlest pig think when he hears the Wolf at the door?

- Let's see how the straw house can be blown away.

- How fast does the littlest pig run when he is chased by the Wolf?

- Does the Wolf catch the littlest pig?

- How does the middle pig feel when he hears the youngest pig's story?

- Do they think they are safe in a house of sticks?

- How hard does the Wolf need to blow to blow down the stick house?

- If you are the stick house, can I see you blow down?

- Does the Wolf almost catch the youngest and middle pigs?

- Do the pigs feel safe in the brick house?

- Can the Wolf blow down the brick house?

- What if the Wolf tries really hard to blow it down?

- How smart was the oldest pig to use bricks to make his house?

- What do the three pigs do when they hear the Wolf on the roof?

- If you are a bubbling pot, how loudly can you bubble and boil?

- How do we pretend that the Wolf comes down the chimney?

- What happens when the Wolf lands in the bubbling pot?

Exploration

"The Three Little Pigs" is a favorite children's story and is great fun to dramatize. It is a very well-known story due to its universality and longevity. This classic story begins with Mother and her three pig children. Once again, there is no father in this story. The mother pig is the sole caretaker. Three, the number of child pigs, is actually a commonly utilized number in children's literature. Examples include "The Three Little Pigs,"

"Goldilocks and the Three Bears," and "The Three Blind Mice," to name a few.

The significance of the opening scene lies in Mother telling her children for the first time that they must go out into the big, wide world on their own. This moment is profound in that everyone faces a time when he or she must "leave the nest" to live on his or her own. This may cause separation anxiety in some children, so it is interesting to see a child's reaction to this particular scenario.

There are three children pigs in this story: the youngest, the middle, and the oldest pig. They become known as the Straw Pig, the Stick Pig, and the Brick Pig. The third and oldest pig is described as the smartest pig due to his wise choice in building materials: bricks. The oldest pig is also the most popular pig to role-play. If working with a group, there may need to be more than one oldest pig selected during the casting process.

After the pigs leave home, one by one they meet an unscrupulous salesman. He is essentially a con artist with no scruples, as he sells materials to the first and second pigs to build a house that he knows full well are substandard. Nevertheless, one by one, he takes the pigs' money, which Mother had given them with a warning to spend wisely.

The first and youngest pig buys straw from the salesman. The straw, sticks, and bricks in the story can actually be played by the children if they would like. Some children like pretending to become a straw house that is eventually blown down by a Wolf. Conversely, some children like becoming the strong brick house that cannot be blown down. Once the straw is purchased, we find out that the youngest pig is quite lazy and literally throws the house together with little, if any, effort. If a child doesn't take on the role of the straw, it can easily be pantomimed. The second (middle) pig buys sticks and again throws together a shoddy house, in part due to his lazy ways. As the story goes, the oldest, wisest, and most industrious pig buys bricks with which to build his house. He is a hard worker and spends much time building a truly strong and safe house.

Once the three pigs have built their three individual houses, the story takes off. A sneaky, cunning, and hungry Wolf comes knocking on the first pig's door. The Wolf can pantomime a knocking motion in the air while the narrator or another child actually makes the knocking sound on a hard surface to coincide with the Wolf's knocking motion.

The pig says, "Who is it?" as he can't see the Wolf and should pretend that he can't.

The Wolf says, "Little pig, little pig, let me in, let me in."

To which the pig replies, "Not by the hair of my chinny chin chin."

And the Wolf replies, "Then I'll huff and puff and blow your house in."

This famous interchange of dialogue repeats itself throughout the story each time the Wolf comes to a pig's house. Children love to repeat this dialogue, in part due to its confrontational nature and also because of the impending chase. Children like repetition in familiar stories, and this is no exception.

Once the Wolf blows down the first house, the scared pig runs for his life. If a child plays the part of the straw house, he or she can be blown away. Otherwise, after the Wolf huffs and puffs, the pig runs and the chase begins. An actual chase can ensue, or you can utilize a slow-motion chase if it is deemed better to control the action somewhat. Also, a game of tag can be incorporated, with the Wolf trying to tag the first little pig, which he may not catch. The first pig runs to the second pig's house unscathed. The scenario repeats itself. The Wolf's threats to blow down the house again become realized as the stick house goes down. Children love the imaginary excitement of being in a presumably safe home one minute and running for their very lives the next. The Wolf, in trying to eat the pigs, is evoking a fear of bodily harm or death in the roles of the pigs. "How did the pig feel when he saw his house being blown to smithereens?" the leader might ask during the postplay review. Children may enjoy pretending to be scared as long as happy resolutions result in the end. It actually can strengthen a child's core.

The Big Bad Wolf represents greed, guile, and bestial carnivorous yearnings. As in any of the other stories in this book containing a wolf, a pack may be created, depending on the casting desires of the participating children. A pack of wolves doesn't affect the plot or structure of the story. If one needs to add more pigs to the story, it is more helpful to add an additional pig to the predetermined trio. So you may create two Brick Pigs, which keeps the story line intact. You may opt to add a fourth or fifth pig to the story, with their own choice of building materials, but this approach tends to lengthen the story considerably and in doing so might cause a loss of the group's attention.

The Wolf's huffing and puffing can be exaggerated for effect. As the stick house gets blown to bits, off run the youngest and middle pigs as fast as they can for the safety of the oldest pig's house. The two younger pigs are depending on the wisdom of their oldest brother (or sister). Once the pigs are inside the brick house, the story repeats itself, but this time, try as he might, the Wolf cannot blow down this house. The younger pigs are a bit scared, but their oldest brother assures them that they are safe inside the brick house. There is a moment of sibling unity. But the antagonist of the story is not too easily defeated, as the Wolf decides to climb up to the rooftop and down through the chimney. The oldest pig hears the Wolf on the roof and quickly gets a pot to place in the fireplace. A child or children may become the bubbling pot. As the story goes, the Wolf lands in the bubbling pot, and everyone lives happily ever after. It is important that the Wolf meet his demise so that a feeling of security and well-being is given back to the pigs.

The themes of the story include growing up and going out on one's own, leaving home for the first time, and the need to feel safe in doing so. Also, work ethic is explored without being overly preachy. The moral of the story need not be repeated, as the point of working hard to have a safe home is implicit in the tale. The strength of family is also explored, which can be touched upon during the processing time.

Tips

- Mother Pig gives each of the Three Little Pigs some money as they leave home. This can easily be pantomimed.

- Most children like to be the Brick Pig or "smartest" pig. More than one child can be this pig, or you can perform the story again, letting someone else have a turn.

- A child can be the straw and stick houses, or you can pantomime them.

- The salesman is a bit of a con artist but fun to play.

- The littlest pig throws his straw house together in a snap.

- The middle pig throws his house of sticks together in a snap.

- The oldest and smartest pig takes time to build a strong house.

- The Wolf is sneaky and hungry and goes straight to the straw house.

- The exchange between the Wolf and the pigs, "Little pig, little pig, let me in!" "Not by the hair of my chinny chin chin!" is infamous and fun for children to act out due to its familiarity and the building of suspense.

- The huffing and puffing of the Wolf can be prolonged by taking two big inhales followed by one big exhale for effect.

- If a child or children are playing the part of the straw house, they can scatter across the room as they get blown away, exposing the vulnerable littlest pig.

- As the Wolf chases the littlest pig, they can actually run, space permitting, or do a slow-motion running in place. The Wolf should not catch the pig.

- The littlest pig will run for his life to the middle pig's house of sticks. There he is safe, albeit just for a few moments.

- Children love the repetition that is often found in children's literature, and "The Three Little Pigs" is no exception.

- The story repeats itself at the Stick Pig's house. Huffing and puffing, the Wolf blows away the house, and the chase begins.

- The oldest pig offers safety and reassurance to his younger siblings. They will all be safe in the brick house.

- The Wolf repeats his huffing and puffing, each time becoming louder and more forceful, yet try as he may, the brick house doesn't budge.

- As the Wolf climbs up onto the roof, which the child playing the Wolf can pretend to do, the pigs get the bubbling pot and place it under the chimney.

- A child or children can pretend to be the bubbling pot in order to catch the Wolf.

- Once the Wolf gets caught in the bubbling pot, he is no longer a threat, and the pigs can celebrate with a song and dance.

Table 9.1. Summary of Story Elements

	"The Three Little Pigs"
Characters	Mother Pig, Straw Pig, Stick Pig, Brick Pig, Salesman, Wolf
Inanimate Roles	Straw, sticks, bricks
Location	Mother's home, wide world, three houses
Timeline	Long ago and far away
Difficulty	Moderate
Length	Medium
Props	Straw, sticks, bricks
Costumes	Four pig ears and tails, wolf ears and tails, hat and vest
Set	Houses
Theme	Out into wide world, industriousness vs. laziness
Plot	Repetition—leaving home, running for safety, happy ending
Emotions	Fear vs. feeling safe
Conflict Resolution	Smartest brother saves siblings and destroys Wolf
Pace	Quick—running
Moral	Hard work pays off

The best-known part of "The Three Little Pigs" is the huffing and puffing scenes, followed by the chase scenes. Again, a story filled with repetition is enjoyable for children. "The Three Little Pigs" is fun, high energy, and familiar for children to play act. The bubbling pot in "The Three Little Pigs" is pivotal in the wolf's demise, but in our next story, the bubbling pot brings about fun and excitement for an entire village!

Notes

1. James Orchard Halliwell-Phillipps, *Popular Rhymes and Nursery Tales: A Sequel to Nursery Rhymes of England* (London: John Russell Smith, 1849).
2. Joseph Jacobs, *English Fairy Tales* (London: David Nutt, 1890).

THE POT THAT
WOULD NOT STOP BOILING

"The Pot That Would Not Stop Boiling" is a less familiar tale recorded by the Brothers Grimm in the nineteenth century. This originally German folktale is short and humorous, yet magical. Several modern versions are readily available today. Other titles for this story include "The Magic Porridge Pot" and "Sweet Porridge." This enchanting tale is retold here in a form that lends itself to dramatization.

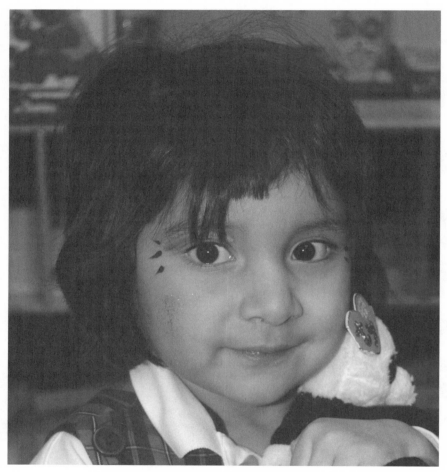

"The pot is a magic porridge pot?" asked the little girl.

The Story

Once upon a time, a long time ago and very far away, there lived a mother and her young daughter. They lived together in a little cottage in a small village, and they were very poor. One day, the mother asked her daughter to go out into the woods to pick some berries so that they would have something to eat. The young girl agreed and skipped off to the woods in search of some berries. No sooner did she start to pick some berries than an old woman appeared before her and asked her what she was doing all alone in the woods.

"Little girl, little girl," the old woman cried, "what are you doing in the woods all alone?"

The little girl stopped picking berries and told the old woman her sad story. Upon hearing this, the old woman paused and then pulled out a small black pot from under her cloak.

"This is a magic pot," said the old woman. "Whenever you are hungry, just say to it, 'Cook, little pot, cook!' and you will have all the sweet porridge of which you could ever dream. Then, when you are done, just say, 'Stop, little pot, stop!' and it will stop. You will never be hungry again. Goodbye, my dear."

And with that, she was gone, leaving the little girl standing alone in the woods, holding the little black pot. She was so excited that she ran home to show her mother, dropping the berry pail behind her. "Mother, Mother! Look what I have!" cried the little girl.

"Oh, is it berries?" asked the mother.

"No," said the little girl.

"Did you find some elderberries?"

"No, Mother, look! It is a magic pot!"

"Oh, daughter, no. What have you done now?"

The girl showed her mother what she had and how it worked. The little black pot was a huge hit, and Mother grew ever so excited. They said, "Cook, little pot, cook!" and the pot magically filled with warm, sweet porridge. It was all that they could eat. Then, they simply said, "Stop, little pot, stop," and the pot stopped boiling.

Well, one day, the little girl went out to play and left Mother at home alone with the magic pot. Mother felt hungry. "Hmmm," she thought, "should I have a bit of porridge? It would taste so good." With that, she took the pot and commanded it to start. "Cook, little pot, cook!" she called. And it did. "No more, little pot, no more!" the mother said, but the little pot continued to boil. "Never mind, little pot. . . . Halt, little pot . . . enough, I said!" she yelled at the pot. But no matter what she said, the pot continued to boil, and soon it bubbled over the edge of the rim. Then it bubbled onto the table and onto the floor. The hot, creamy porridge bubbled right out of the door. The mother continued to yell, "Quit it, no more, just cut it out, little pot!" But she had forgotten the magic words, so the pot continued to bubble and boil. Out of the door went the porridge, and it poured into the street. Suddenly, there was a river of porridge rolling down the road. She couldn't stop it, try as she might.

All of the people in the village came out of their cottages to see what all the commotion was about. Even the animals came out from near and from far. There were men, women, and children. There were cows, horses, cats, and dogs, too. Everyone was eating the porridge! And they were all scooping it up in bowls and buckets too! "Yum, yum!" they shouted. As the porridge reached the last house in the village and it started to creep slowly under the door, the little girl, who was playing there, saw it and immediately knew what had happened. She ran home and said, "Stop, little pot, stop!" And it did.

The porridge pot stopped, and do you know that the village people and all of the animals ate porridge for three weeks?

And that is the story of "The Pot That Would Not Stop Boiling."

"Look at all of this porridge!" meowed the cat.

Questions

- How do you know the family is poor?

- Are they hungry? How does it look to be hungry?

- What kind of food did Mother send her daughter to get?

- Can you pretend to pick berries?

- Where can you put them?

- Does anyone want to be the trees in the forest?

- Are your roots firmly planted in the ground?

- How do you move when the breeze blows? Is it a gentle breeze?

- Where can the old woman be hiding?

- Is the girl startled to see her?

- Can you pretend to be startled?

- How does the old woman walk and talk? Is she scary or kind?

- Why does the woman give the girl the pot?

- If some of you are pretending to be the pot, how would you sit or stand together to form the pot?

- Does Mother believe it is a magic pot?

- If you were the porridge inside of the pot, how would you bubble up to the brim without spilling over the edge?

- What are the magic words to make the pot start?

- What are the magic words to make the pot stop?

- If you are the mother or the girl, can I see you pretending to eat your porridge very hungrily?

- How many bowls of porridge can you eat?

- How can you show us that you are full?

- This time, when Mother starts the pot, she can't stop it. Why not?

- What are some other words for "stop"? Remember, you can't say "stop."

- Let's see the bubbly porridge flow out of the door and down the street like a river.

- How would you move if you were a river of porridge?

- If you are a villager, can you pretend to grab a bucket and scoop up some porridge?

- If you are a village animal, can you eat some porridge? There is plenty for everyone.

- How hungry are you?

- How does the sweet porridge taste?

- When does the girl know that there is a problem?

- What does the girl say to the pot when she gets home?

- How long does it take the villagers to eat the porridge in the street?

- Let's see how long it takes you to eat up all the porridge.

Exploration

"The Pot That Would Not Stop Boiling" begins with a mother and a young daughter living in a small cottage. There is no mention of a father, just like in "The Boy Who Cried Wolf" and "The Three Little Pigs." There is not enough food to eat, as they are very poor. The level of poverty is reminiscent of "Hansel and Gretel." Both characters are nameless and therefore timeless. Just like in "Little Red Riding Hood," Mother sends her daughter into the woods, although this time with a better outcome.

Children can be the trees in the forest. Allow them to securely plant their feet as the roots hold them fast to the floor. They can't move their feet once they are in place. Their arms can be the branches. When a gentle breeze blows, their arms can sway gently. The children who play the trees make up the forest collectively. They should see whether they can hold their faces very still and neutral. As a chorus, they could even comment on the story like a voice in the wind.

The young girl finds some berries in the woods and pantomimes picking them and placing them in her pail. As she partakes in this activity, an old woman appears. The old woman may be portrayed as a witch if you choose. She is magical and turns out to be a good character. She can be hiding behind a tree before she makes herself known. The audience can see her before the young girl sees her, which adds suspense. Having the audience know something that the primary character does not creates the sense of being "in on" something.

Once the old woman hears of the girl's sad plight, she offers her a wonderful gift that she has hidden beneath her cloak. If a child or children are pretending to be the magical pot, they can simply hide behind the old woman until she presents the pot to the girl. The character of the old woman is mysterious and generous, considering that the girl earned the pot without performing good deeds or exchanging something of value. In "Jack and the Beanstalk," an exchange between Jack and the mysterious man takes place when Jack trades his cow for magic beans.

Just as quickly as the old woman appears out of nowhere, she disappears behind one of the trees. The girl now has the magic pot; presumably, she will never go hungry. She will never want for anything. Endless sweet porridge is more than she could have ever dreamed.

Once she gets home, a guessing game can ensue as Mother tries to guess what her daughter has brought home. Children love guessing games. Improvise this freely with the children's ideas. Notice that Mother starts to get angry when she realizes that her daughter came home with no berries. Mother can indicate this anger with her posture and her voice. Children know how to pretend to be angry, and it is fun for them to try on this extreme emotion.

The girl finally shows her mother the pot, and of course, Mother doesn't believe for one minute that it is magical. Moreover, Mother does not like the fact that her daughter had been talking to a strange old woman in the woods. However, when the girl says the magic command, the porridge begins to boil! Children who are the porridge can start to wriggle and pop but are still contained within the imaginary pot (or the children making up the sides of the pot).

Children love being bubbly porridge. They can best equate porridge to today's oatmeal. Give the children playing porridge a chance to move slowly and practice growing and expanding. They do not flow over the sides of the pot yet. The children can add bubbling and boiling sounds, too.

Meanwhile, mother and daughter can pantomime eating yummy and delicious porridge. They have been so ravenous that they can eat many bowlfuls. They should eat using an imaginary spoon and bowl until they feel full. Children enjoy eating even when it is through pretend play. It actually develops feelings of security and nurturance.

One day, the girl leaves the house and Mother is home alone. Mother debates whether to have some porridge or not, as she is hungry and the sweet porridge is so tempting. It is a funny moment for the audience to see the mother debating to herself, "Should I or shouldn't I have some porridge?" This is particularly true when she gives in to temptation, to which most people can relate. Mother commands the pot to start, much to her delight, but when she tries to stop the pot, she cannot. This is role reversal in that usually it is the child who gets into trouble, especially when home alone! The children playing the porridge slowly yet increasingly bubble and boil, although this time, give them permission to bubble over the pot. Children playing the pot itself can drop hands or fall to the ground as the porridge rolls away. This scene is climactic and very fun for the children.

Part of the story's appeal is the underlying theme of overabundance and a loss of control. The story signifies a letting go. The porridge overflowing is the pivotal point in the story, when there is too much of a good thing, and everything begins to run amok. Children love to be a warm, gooey, and mushy substance. It is regressive yet fun. As the porridge, children bubble out of the pot, and they can literally roll or crawl as they spread everywhere. First, they go out of the pot, then across the floor and right out the door. It is easier not to involve the use of a table in order to keep all of the young actors on the ground. The porridge children should be moving in very slow motion in order to maintain some control of a potentially chaotic scene. You will have to set some boundaries and parameters ahead of time so that the children will not run into one another physically. Let them practice this scene before doing the whole story with no touching, bumping, or physical contact with one another. The beauty of this story is that children can be runaway porridge from an out-of-control pot within a controlled environment simply by establishing guidelines.

Meanwhile, Mother is calling out a host of commands in her futile attempt to stop the pot: "Never!" "Halt!" "No more!" "Finish!" "Enough!" "Quit it!" Children can help think of similar commands without saying, "Stop, little pot, stop!"

Now cue the ensemble of assorted villagers to come out to the street as the porridge rolls by like a river. Cue them verbally or point to them to enter the acting area. You can say, "And out came the villagers." Then give the children a nod of your head, using eye contact with them as needed. The people can bring imaginary spoons, buckets, or bowls to fill, and the animals just eat from the porridge's edge, like drinking from a river. Again, no physical contact is required or needed for this action.

Children in the roles of villagers and village animals can be any type of person, farm animal, pet, or stray, as long as they appear to delight in the porridge river. One child may want to be a purple sparkle unicorn, and someone else may want to be a cuddly baby. The mood is high because the food is free and abundant. Everyone is hungry, but as they eat the porridge, they hunger no more. In actuality, it is a rags-to-riches story. The porridge has become a flowing river filling the imaginary street. The villagers can improvise fun dialogue as they discover the yummy porridge and gobble it up.

As the porridge makes its way down to the last house on the street, the little girl playing there sees the porridge and because she is the daughter immediately recognizes what happened. She runs home and stops the pot with the magic command. As the story ends, the villagers and the animals are still indulging in the seemingly endless porridge.

Tips

- As the story begins, mother and daughter are very poor, and very hungry too. This can be reflected by a low, sad mood.

- The children playing the trees in the forest should have their feet planted firmly on the ground as if they were rooted.

- A gentle breeze can blow the trees' branches (children's arms).

- A tree's face can be neutral and expressionless. See which child can hold his face still the best!

- The girl can pantomime the picking of berries using no props.

- The old woman (witch) is hiding behind one of the trees.

- The witch in this story turns out not to be a mean witch but a kind old woman.

- The audience can see the old woman hiding behind the tree, but the girl cannot see her.

- The girl is very humble and sweet in sharing her story with the old woman.

- A child or children can be the magic porridge pot.

- The pot can hide behind the old woman until she reveals her surprise.

- After the old woman gives the pot to the girl and tells her the commands, she disappears again behind a tree.

- The little girl is now happy and excited to run home to show her mother.

- Mother and daughter can play a brief guessing game to determine the surprise that the girl has now hidden from her mother.

- Mother is upset at first until she sees the pot in action.

- Children who are the porridge can wriggle and pop inside of the pot as it is activated.

- The porridge can grow and expand, but in slow motion.

- At this point, the porridge bubbles and boils, yet stays in the pot.

- The porridge can have bubbling and boiling sounds.

- Mother and daughter can pantomime eating countless bowls of porridge. No bowls or spoons are necessary.

- Mother is home alone one day and commands the pot to start boiling. While she is happily eating porridge, she tries to stop the pot and quickly realizes she can't.

- At this point, the porridge slowly begins to roll out of the pot.

- The children can help think of various commands to stop the pot without saying, "Stop, little pot, stop!" They might say, "Never, halt, no more, finish, enough, quit it, cut it out!"

- Meanwhile, the pot itself can drop hands and fall away so that the porridge can escape.

- The porridge goes onto the floor and out of the door.

- Most children love pretending to be mushy, gooey, and overflowing porridge.

- You may want to practice this porridge scene ahead of time.

- Once the porridge rolls into the street, the villagers and assorted animals come out.

- Cue the entrance of the villagers and animals by using words or a signal, such as a nod of your head.

- The villagers and animals are hungry and can say this aloud. They begin to eat the river of porridge without actually touching it.

- The villagers can use imaginary bowls or buckets to scoop up the porridge.

- Children can become any person or animal that they can think of, such as mother, father, child, horse, cow, cat, or dog.

- The mood is high because everyone has been hungry, and now the villagers and animals are all eating.

- The villagers can create improvised dialogue, and the animals can add animal sounds.

- Finally, the little girl sees the runaway porridge and knows immediately what has happened.

- The girl runs home and commands the pot to stop, and the pot goes back to its original form and stops boiling.

- The porridge pot stops, and the whole village continues to eat happily as the story ends.

Table 10.1. Summary of Story Elements

"The Pot That Would Not Stop Boiling"	
Characters	Mother, girl, old woman, villagers, assorted animals
Inanimate Roles	The pot, the porridge
Location	A cottage, small village, the woods
Timeline	Long ago and far away
Difficulty	Simple
Length	Short
Props	n/a
Costumes	Apron, shawl
Set	N/A
Theme	Overabundance, bubbling out of control
Plot	Rags to riches
Emotions	Hunger, satisfaction, out of control
Conflict Resolution	A happy ending after a near disaster
Pace	Steady, then overflows
Moral	Too much of a good thing is not so good

"The Pot That Would Not Stop Boiling" is a clever folktale that is perfect fun for all ages to dramatize. Some children actually become the never-ending bubbling pot, while others become the rolling porridge stream that rolls across the floor and out the door. This centuries-old tale remains fresh today because it has the physical action that kids love.

IMAGINATION: PRACTICE FOR LIVING

"**M**y child loves it!" says the mother to me regarding the drama program. "Oh, thank you!" I say. "No, I mean she *really* loves it," Mother insists. "That is so nice to hear," I say. "Every morning when she wakes up she asks if this is the day she will have drama." Gratifyingly, I have received this feedback repeatedly over the years, and it remains refreshing.

"Imagination improves language, creativity, and the ability to solve problems."[1] What's more, imagination allows a child to try on new roles and in the process expands the child's own identity and perspectives on life. By becoming various characters, a child develops more depth in his or her own persona. This includes expanding a child's ability to empathize and understand others' plights. The new experiences explored through play acting become etched in the child's repertoire of life experiences. The pretend interactions of dramatic play help prepare a child to interact in real-life scenarios. After all, if a child can defeat a witch using his or her own wit and wisdom, facing a daily obstacle such as dealing with a bully on the bus may not be so hard.

The benefits of encouraging a child's imagination are extensive. As we have explored, imagination greatly enhances the following:

- socialization

- interaction

- communication

And they lived happily ever after.

- sensory awareness

- emotional expressiveness

- creativity

- cooperation and teamwork

Plus, it is *fun*!

In helping children to imagine and pretend, one is paving the way to an adjusted and fulfilled adulthood. Research indicates that children who are imaginative and creative will grow to become successful adults.[2] By following the guidelines outlined in this book, a parent or teacher can shape and develop a child today to promote excellence for tomorrow.

The Story Drama Method has been developed and refined over the past two decades. The structure of the method has guided literally hundreds, if not thousands, of children in creating their own interpretation of stories, and it continues today. Child Drama Workshops, my theatre arts enrichment program, serves more than four hundred children annually in Delaware and Pennsylvania schools utilizing this method on a daily basis. Established in 1994, the program allows professional actor-educators to encourage the use of creativity and imagination in children ages three through nine, with drama as the vehicle. The program flourishes in the schools (both private and public), community centers, and resource centers. Child Drama Workshops programs are rooted in artistic and educational means.

The Story Drama Method is simple and doable, yet it has broad implications for improving a child's development. All that is needed is a space, an individual child or children, and a story. The audience is actually optional, depending upon predetermined goals. As the leader reads, tells, or acts out the story and the children listen, their imaginative processes begin. For this reason, it is preferable not to use a book or show pictures so that children can create images in their mind based on the auditory telling of the story. If the leader simply acts out the story, the child can observe the choice of characters from which to draw. After the story is told, often children can barely maintain their composure, raising their hands enthusiastically so that they can select the part they want to play. "I wanna be . . ." they shout. Let them be whoever or whatever they choose. In following the techniques of the method, the creative process unfolds. Use the tips for each individual story to promote a quality experience for everyone.

One cannot fully describe how wonderful it is to see children pretending to be someone or something of their own choosing in a story drama. When they are wholly engaged in the act of imagining, everyone is transported to another time and place. They become part of the story. The children inject life into characters and objects that would otherwise lie dormant in the pages of a book.

The delight that results from experiencing this world of imagination is revealed in scene after scene in these stories. The sheer joy of chase scenes illuminates the young faces. When the Big Bad Wolf is defeated, jumping up and down shows that the children feel the victory. The children all celebrate the sensation of freedom when Hansel is liberated from the locked cage. Each of these heartfelt emotions are played out and explored in this world full of discovery. The children literally cheer for a happy ending for each story, as they so deserve. With adoring applause from a supportive audience, the child's satisfaction is complete. Indeed, the audience shares the positive emotions elicited by the ensemble.

Even when the performance does not completely go as planned, the unforeseen slip-ups that occur make for the most endearing moments to the audience. The three-year-old king announces his proclamation to the village only to have his crown slowly slide over his eyes. The wolf tries to catch the billy goat only to find himself with the Velcro tail in his paw. The prince grimaces during what was supposed to be a tender moment with the princess. These moments simply add to the enjoyment with the spontaneity and unpredictability of child actors in a live play. Anything can happen, and anything will happen. That is why it is important to have the solid foundation and practices that this book provides in place—to accommodate the unknown.

When I was an adolescent, my younger brother was cast in the leading role of Santa Claus in his elementary school play. The teacher most likely assigned the role to him because he was such a good student—the Santa Claus character had the most lines in the script. He became overwhelmed at the task of memorizing so many lines. He had feelings of self-doubt and despair. He believed there was no way he could remember all of those lines. He had never done anything such as this before, and he was literally in tears. To help him overcome his fears, I practiced lines with him repeatedly until he was confident. I later learned that his anxiety was exacerbated by the crush he had on the female classmate playing Mrs. Claus, not to mention that the premise of the play was that Santa's pants were at the cleaners and Christmas might have been cancelled due to a wardrobe malfunction. This meant that most of the play would require him to be onstage in a bathrobe—sans pants!

Although my brother went on to ace that performance, I became convinced that scripts should not be used with young children. As I studied theatre, I learned that acting without scripts is standard practice in Great Britain, where drama is a part of every elementary school curriculum. In the field of educational theatre there, they have found that, as I believe, it is not necessary to have young children memorize lines when they can readily improvise using their own words and imaginations. As part of this practice, and in my Story Drama Method, the instructor needs to be comfortable letting go so that the magic can happen. The results are priceless.

There are so many issues that children are facing today: childhood obesity, broken marriages and homes, autism—and all of this in an economic climate where both parents must work, often at multiple jobs. There is no better time to offer all children a chance to explore their day-to-day societal, familial, and developmental struggles through characters in the ageless and universal literature found in this book, giving every child a chance to imagine and to create in order that they can succeed as unique individuals. Creativity and imagination are key components in childhood development, which translates into a well-adjusted adult life.

Through the use of imagination, one can be anything and go anywhere without leaving the living room or classroom. A child can be the Gingerbread Man running gleefully through the fields, taunting all who try to catch him. Another child can be the river running through the same story, lapping up against the cookie's feet. The Story Drama Method goes beyond the benefits of reading to children by bringing the story to life and enriching children's lives in the process. It quickly becomes practice for living. There is no doubt when looking into the children's faces that the wonderment and awe inspired by the tales triggers the imagination.

Notes

1. Helen F. Neville, *Is This a Phase? Child Development & Parent Strategies, Birth to 6 Years* (Seattle: Parenting Press, 2009), 155.
2. Sandra W. Russ, Andrew L. Robins, and Beth A. Christiano, "Pretend Play: Longitudinal Prediction of Creativity and Affect in Fantasy in Children," *Creativity Research Journal* 12, no. 2 (1987): 129–39.

APPENDIX A
Suggested Stories for the Story Drama Method

Irecommend the following stories for play acting. They are easily accessible and familiar tales as well. I have used each of the stories listed for many years in the classroom because they lend themselves to dramatization.

Brett, Jan. *The Mitten*. New York: Putnam, 1989.

Brown, Marsha. *Three Billy Goats Gruff*. Orlando, FL: Voyager, 1957.

Flack, Marjorie. *Ask Mr. Bear*. New York: Simon & Schuster Children's Publishing, 1971.

Fuller, Muriel, ed. "Goldilocks and the Three Bears," in *Favorite Old Fairy Tales*. New York: Nelson, 1949.

Gág, Wanda. *Millions of Cats*. New York: Coward-McCann, 1928.

Grimm, Jacob Ludwig Carl, and Wilhelm Carl Grimm. *Rumpelstiltskin*. New York: Avenel, 1981.

Grimm, Jacob Ludwig Carl, and Wilhelm Carl Grimm. *The Straw, the Bean and the Coal*. New York: Avenel, 1981.

The Little Red Hen. New York: Golden Books, 1954.

Slobodkina, Esphyr. *Caps for Sale*. New York: Harper Collins, 1987.

APPENDIX B
Accessories/Props

Props, costume accessories, or the occasional set piece can be considered if doing a play presentation for an audience. The story dramatizations that are described in this book require no materials. Props, accessories, or a set piece are all able to be imagined.

Most props are best created by pantomime or pretend. If you choose to use an occasional prop, it should be introduced late in the process. Most simple props can be found around the home. If you decide to use props, they would be best saved for just before a presentation to an audience. You should rehearse with any new prop at least once before a presentation since props often allow inadvertent mistakes to happen.

Set pieces, such as a tree or a river, are usually represented by the young actors themselves or by the leader. An occasional chair can be used to set the placement for a door or a kitchen space as needed.

The costume accessories can be used over and over again from story to story. You can buy them online or make simple animal ears and tails. Feather boas make nice bird wings. An assortment of hats, vests, and big scraps of material is really all that is needed.

Less is more in allowing the child to use his or her imagination. The following is a list of what you may need.

The Wolf and the Seven Kids

Set Pieces

- Door—Use a chair to represent the door to the house
- Lake—A child can play this part, or a large blue piece of material can be used as the lake
- Tree—To be played by the instructor or a child who volunteers

Costumes

- Goats—Goat ears and tails, bell necklaces (use ribbon and bells from a craft store), goatees (optional—use polyfill and spirit gum)
- Wolf—Wolf ears and tail
- Baker—Apron and hat

The Gingerbread Man

Set Pieces

- Oven—Generally a pantomime oven
- River—Can be blue material, or use children as the rippling, splashing river

Costumes

- Old Lady—Apron, wig, or scarf
- Old Man—Hat or vest
- Workmen—Hats or vests
- Cow—Ears, tail
- Horse—Ears, tail
- Fox—Ears, tail

Little Red Riding Hood

Set Pieces

- Woods—Can use children as trees
- Bed—Set up a couple of chairs

Props

- Basket (optional)

Costumes

- Mother—Apron
- Little Red Riding Hood—Red cape, dress all in red, or use a red blanket
- Wolf—Ears and tail
- Grandmother—Nightgown and cap

The Boy Who Cried Wolf

Set Pieces

- Kitchen—Use a chair for the breakfast table
- Rock in field—Use a chair for the rock (optional)

Costumes

- Mom—Apron
- Boy—Vest and/or cap
- Sheep—Ears and tails, bells on ribbon for neck (optional)
- Wolf—Ears and tail

Jack and the Beanstalk

Set Pieces

- Beanstalk—Easier to pantomime, or you could build it using cardboard and green leaves.

Costumes

- Mother—Apron
- Jack—Vest and/or cap
- Cow—Ears and tail
- Salesman—Cap and vest
- Giant—Oversized clothes stuffed with a pillow
- Giant's Wife—Oversized clothes stuffed with a pillow
- Hen—Feathered boa wrapped around arms and neck for use as wings
- Harp—Gold clothes and strings

The Lion and the Mouse

Props

- Net—It is more fun for someone to be the net, but you can use an actual net or a blanket.

Costumes

- Lion—Ears or mane and tail
- Mouse—Ears and tail
- Men—Vests and/or hats

Hansel and Gretel

Props

- Breadcrumbs—Can pantomime, or use popcorn
- Bone—Pantomime, or use a dog bone
- Jewels—Pantomime, or use costume necklace/jewels

Costumes

- Father—Old clothes, torn and tattered
- Stepmother—Old clothes, torn and tattered
- Hansel—Vest and cap
- Gretel—Poor dress
- Witch—Hat, cape, witch-type dress
- Birds—Feather boa for wings

Three Little Pigs

Set Pieces

- Houses of straw, sticks, and bricks—It is most creative to have a child in the role of the straw house, stick house, and brick house. The child is first introduced by the salesman as straw, sticks, or bricks. Another option is to use cardboard or cardboard boxes and decorate them accordingly.

Costumes

- Mom—Ears, tail, and apron
- Straw Pig—Ears, tail, and vest
- Stick Pig—Ears, tail, and vest
- Brick Pig—Ears, tail, and vest

- Salesman—Vest or coat and hat
- Wolf—Ears and tail

The Pot That Would Not Stop Boiling

Set Pieces

- Home/Kitchen—Use a folding chair in the kitchen
- Forest—Trees can be played by children
- Stream of porridge—played by children

Costumes

- Mother—Old, torn clothes
- Girl—Old, torn clothes
- Villagers—Old assorted hats/vests
- Assorted animals—Ears/tails

APPENDIX C
Theatre Games and Warm-ups

Many good books of theatre games are available for children. Below are a few games that work particularly well with young children.

What's Different?

Everyone sits in a circle. A child volunteers to be "it" and go first, and he or she stands up so that all can see him or her. The child tells everyone his or her name and age. Everyone observes the child very closely. Then they all put their heads down and close their eyes. While all children hide their eyes, the child who is "it" changes one thing about how he or she looks. For example, the child could untie one shoelace, unbutton one button, roll up one sleeve, take off a ponytail holder, and so on. The leader may need to help get the ball rolling. For fun, the leader can add her own sunglasses to the child or bring in a hat. To vary the game as you go along, two children can volunteer at once to be "it." Another child can also be chosen to be the one to make a change on the child who is "it." Then, to vary it further, two changes can be made per child. The slight changes during the game help hold the children's interest and encourage creative thinking.

What's Missing?

Simply bring in ten objects of an assorted nature (for example, clothespin, small doll, block, pinecone), and place them in front of the children to observe. After a moment or two, have the children close their eyes as you remove one object. Then let them open their eyes. Allow the children to raise their hands if they know what item is missing. Remind them not to call out the answer. This gives other children a chance to find the answer. Variations include removing more than one item and rearranging remaining items while their eyes are closed. Then another child can remove an item or two.

Nursery Rhyme Time

A nursery rhyme can be a wonderfully short and simple yet fun story to act out.[1] Start by reciting a nursery rhyme from beginning to end. For example:

> Jack be nimble,
> Jack be quick,
> Jack jump over the candlestick.

One person is to be Jack. One person is the candlestick. Jack leaps over the candlestick. Just be sure the candle is always hunched down low so that Jack can make a clear leap. This can then be repeated so that two more children can take a turn.

> Little Miss Muffet
> Sat on a tuffet
> Eating her curds and whey.
> Along came a spider
> And sat down beside her
> And frightened Miss Muffet away.

One child is to be Miss Muffet. One child can be the tuffet (Miss Muffet doesn't actually sit on the tuffet with her full weight, but rather can lean gently upon him or her). One child volunteers to be the spider. The spider enters and sits. Miss Muffet runs away, screaming. This rhyme is short and fun filled, and it contains lots of emotion. Recast and do it again. Always let the children be who they choose, not who you choose them to be. Children enjoy acting out these rhymes, especially if the instructor acts with them for the first or second time. Other favorites include "Jack and Jill," "Hickory Dickory Dock," and "Four and Twenty Blackbirds."

Follow the Leader

In this version, the leader—the instructor—selects a character from the story of the day and leads the line while moving like that character. For example, in "The Lion and the Mouse," the line might move like the Lion. Then add sound to the movements. Next, the leader becomes the Mouse. Have everyone move like a mouse, and then add sounds. This game can be personalized for each story so that the children can practice developing the characters together as a group. They can even be the character of the net for "The Lion and the Mouse."

Duck, Duck, Goose

This traditional game can become "Pig, Pig, Wolf" or "Sheep, Sheep, Wolf," complete with animal movements and animal sounds. The variations can be done for any story described in this book. Everyone sits in a circle, and the child who is "it" walks around the exterior of the circle, gently tapping each child on the head while saying, "Duck . . . duck . . . duck." When the child picks someone and says, "Goose," that selected child must stand up and chase the original child around the circle until they get back to the vacated seat. If the child who is "it" makes it back to the opening in the circle without being tagged, then that child is safe. Now the "goose" is "it."

Notes

1. Blanche Fisher Wright, *The Real Mother Goose, Vol. 7* (New York: Scholastic, 1994).

APPENDIX D
Drama with Special-Needs Children

For more information on drama with special-needs children, please refer to my book, *Pediatric Dramatherapy: They Couldn't Run So They Learned to Fly.*[1]

Pediatric Dramatherapy shows how chronically ill children who are unable to verbalize their feelings or inner conflicts can do so through dramatherapy. The major sources of stress for chronically ill children are examined as they relate to situations within selected stories. Through detailed case studies, commentaries, and analysis, this groundbreaking book demonstrates a connection between the child's symbolic expression and the struggle with illness. The use of puppets, masks, makeup, and costume accessories enhances the children's ability for self-expression. This work is a resource for all those working with traumatized children as well as a resource for the emerging field of arts medicine.

I have used dramatherapy successfully with children facing Asperger's syndrome, ADHD, bipolar disorder, Tourette's syndrome, selective mutism, and children dealing with divorce. Please see www.playtherapy delaware.com for more information.

Note

1. Carol E. Bouzoukis, *Pediatric Dramatherapy: They Couldn't Run So They Learned to Fly* (London: Jessica Kingsley, 2001).

BIBLIOGRAPHY

Adams, W. H. Davenport. *Round About Our Coal Fire: Or Christmas Entertainments*, 2nd ed. London: J. Roberts, 1734.

Canning, Natalie, and Michael Reed. *Reflective Practice in the Early Years*. London: Sage, 2009.

Conley, Dalton. "Wired for Distraction?" *Time*, February 21, 2011.

Einstein, Albert. *Cosmic Religion: With Other Opinions and Aphorisms*. New York: Dover, 1931.

"The Gingerbread Boy." *St. Nicholas Magazine,* May 1875.

Grimm, Jacob Ludwig Carl, and Wilhelm Carl Grimm. *Grimms' Fairy Tales: Forty-two Household Tales*. Charleston, SC: Forgotten Books, 2008.

Halliwell-Phillipps, James Orchard. *Popular Rhymes and Nursery Tales: A Sequel to Nursery Rhymes of England*. London: John Russell Smith, 1849.

Jack the Giant Killer. Newcastle, England: J. White, 1711.

Jacobs, Joseph. *English Fairy Tales*. London: David Nutt, 1890.

Karp, Harvey. *The Happiest Toddler on the Block*. New York: Bantam Dell, 2008.

Neville, Helen F. *Is This a Phase? Child Development and Parent Strategies, Birth to 6 Years*. Seattle: Parenting Press, 2007.

Perrault, Charles. *Tales from Past Times, with Morals: Tales of Mother Goose*. New York: D. C. Heath, 1901.

Russ, Sandra W., Andrew L. Robins, and Beth A. Christiano. "Pretend Play: Longitudinal Prediction of Creativity and Affect in Fantasy in Children." *Creativity Research Journal* 12 (1999): 129–39. Accessed March 28, 2011. doi:10.1207/s15326934crj1202_5.

Wright, Blanche Fisher *The Real Mother Goose, Vol. 7*. New York: Scholastic, 1994.

FURTHER READING

Bettelheim, Bruno. *The Uses of Enchantment: The Meaning and Importance of Fairy Tales.* New York: Vintage, 1975.

Bouzoukis, Carol E. *Pediatric Dramatherapy: They Couldn't Run So They Learned to Fly.* London: Jessica Kingsley, 2001.

Brun, Birgitte, Ernst W. Pederson, and Marianne Runberg. *Symbols of the Soul: Therapy and Guidance through Fairy Tales.* London: Jessica Kingsley, 1993.

Courtney, Richard. *Play, Drama & Thought.* New York: Drama Book Specialists, 1974.

Gersie, Alida, and Nancy King. *Storymaking in Education and Therapy.* London: Jessica Kingsley, 1990.

Ginsburg, Kenneth R. "The Importance of Play in Promoting Healthy Child Development and Maintaining Strong Parent-Child Bonds." *American Academy of Pediatrics* 119, no. 1 (2007): 182–90.

Hodgson, John, ed. *The Uses of Drama.* London: Methuen, 1972.

Landy, Robert. *Drama Therapy: Concepts, Theories, and Practices*, 2nd ed. Springfield, IL: Charles C. Thomas, 1994.

MacPherson, Karen. "Experts Concerned about Children's Creative Thinking." *Pittsburgh Post-Gazette*, 2004.

Mallet, Charles. *Fairytales and Children.* New York: Schocken, 1984.

May, Pamela. *Child Development in Practice: Responsive Teaching and Learning from Birth to Five.* New York: Routledge, 2010.

McCaslin, Nellie. *Creative Drama in the Classroom.* New York: Longman, 2006.

Salisburg, Barbara. *Theatre Arts in the Elementary Classroom.* New Orleans: Anchorage Press, 1996.

Siks, Geraldine Brain. *Drama with Children.* New York: Harper & Row, 1983.

FURTHER READING

Slade, Peter. *Child Play: Its Importance for Human Development.* London: Jessica Kingsley, 1995.

Wagner, Betty Jane. *Dorothy Heathcote: Drama as a Learning Medium.* Washington, DC: National Education Association, 1999.

Winnicott, D. W. *Playing & Reality.* London: Tavistock, 2005.

INDEX

ABOUT THE AUTHOR

Carol E. Bouzoukis is a child drama specialist and psychotherapist with more than twenty-five years of experience in encouraging children to use their imaginations. Dr. Bouzoukis is the founder of Child Drama Workshops Ltd., which provides interactive theatre arts enrichment programs to schools in the Wilmington, Delaware, region. Children ages three and up participate in creating new and original performances utilizing the Story Drama Method described in this book. Dr. Bouzoukis also maintains a creative psychotherapy practice, Play Therapy Delaware, treating children with behavioral challenges such as bipolar disorder, Asperger's syndrome, selective mutism, sensory integration disorder, and ADHD. She is the author of *Pediatric Dramatherapy: They Couldn't Run So They Learned to Fly*, which details the use of drama and play as methods of psychological healing for chronically ill children through arts medicine. Dr. Bouzoukis earned her bachelor's degree from Western Maryland College, her master of fine arts degree from the University of North Carolina, and her doctorate from New York University.